Anonymous

The Catholics of Scotland

Vol. 03

Anonymous

The Catholics of Scotland
Vol. 03

ISBN/EAN: 9783743342354

Manufactured in Europe, USA, Canada, Australia, Japa

Cover: Foto ©Lupo / pixelio.de

Manufactured and distributed by brebook publishing software (www.brebook.com)

Anonymous

The Catholics of Scotland

CAP. XXXVI.

CHANGES—MR. JAMES CARRUTHERS—MR. ANDREW DAWSON—PROGRESS—KEMPCAIRN—REPAIRS OF THE "HIGHLAND CHAPEL" OPPOSED—PROCEEDED WITH—ANNUAL MEETING OF 1785—MEASURES PROPOSED—THE COLLEGE AT PARIS—ITS GREAT UTILITY—MR. DORLET—DECLINE OF THE COLLEGE—BETTER PROSPECTS—THE BISHOP DISAPPOINTED—THINKS OF RESIGNING—IN BETTER HEALTH CONTINUES HIS LABOURS—RESTORATION OF THE HIGHLAND CHAPEL COMPLETED—THE PARIS COLLEGE—PRINCIPAL GORDON'S "MEMOIR" ANSWERED—A COMPROMISE.

Changes in the missions were necessarily very frequent. Mr. James Cameron, Chaplain at Kirkconnel, was removed to Aberneen, Mr. Maxwell stipulating that Mr. McGillivray should be sent to supply his place. In compliance, however, with the wishes of Mr. McGillivray's congregation, the Bishop declined to remove him. Finally, Mr. Maxwell's influence prevailed in securing the services of Mr. McGillivray as his Chaplain. Mr. James Cameron was appointed to succeed Mr. Fraser, an ex-Jesuit, in the mission of Munshes, in Galloway, the family

there being still Catholic, and Mr. John Gordon, nephew of Bishop Geddes, replaced Mr. Cameron at Aberdeen. The mission of Glenlivat fell to Mr. James Carruthers, who had just completed his studies at Douai, and who, in his riper years, was known as the author of a History of Scotland, and a vindication of Queen Mary. Mr. William Reid was removed from Shenval to the Stryla mission, of which Keith was the centre; and Mr. Andrew Dawson, afterwards President at Scalan, commenced his missionary career at Shenval, the chief place of the Cabrach district. Such frequent changes were to none more unpleasant than the Bishop; but they could not be avoided. "Necessity," he stated, "has now for many years been our only guide in these matters."

It is indicative of progress that it was appointed for the priest of the Stryla mission to reside at Kempcairn, near Keith, where a chapel and house were to be provided for him. This was not the only missionary establishment that the Bishop was engaged to provide for. He felt the burden; but was resigned. "For my part," he wrote to his coadjutor, "I think my money cannot be better employed than for such a purpose. But I cannot do all, and hope you will do something, at least for Kempcairn." Mr. Reid survived the Bishop fourteen years: and in his latter days, which, like his earlier time, were usefully employed, was known as the "Patriarch."

It became necessary this year to make repairs in the old chapel on the east side of Blackfriars' Wynd. The Bishop could not, on account of other demands upon him, contribute anything towards the expense. He recommended, in consequence, that the funds required should be borrowed; and the interest paid out of the proceeds of the bench rents, and the capital by instalments from time to time. One of the neighbours opposed the repairs, as had been done in the case of the alterations required at the chapel on the opposite side. Mr. Menzies, the priest, promptly sought legal advice; and in two hours from the time the work was stopped, the Dean of Guild and his council were on the top of the walls, hearing what could be said and shown on either side. He decided in favour of continuing the repairs; and the adverse party threatened an appeal to the court of session. But nothing appears to have been done, as the work was continued without any further interruption. This chapel was known as "St. Andrew's Chapel;" but it was sometimes also called the "Highland Chapel," as Mr. Menzies preached in it on Sunday, in Gaelic, to the Highland congregation."

Bishop Hay desired very much that his friend and coadjutor should be present this year, 1785, at the usual annual meeting of the Bishops. Bishop Geddes was by no means disinclined to attend; and lest there should arise any inconvenience in consequence of his absence from Edinburgh, Abbe Paul Macpherson was appointed to do duty for him there. He informed Bishop Hay that he had several measures to propose for the better management of their common affairs. To this the Bishop made no objections, assuring him that he was at full liberty to propose whatever he thought most conducive to the common good ; for he had "nothing more at heart than to see our little community settled upon the most solid footing, that matters may not be exposed to fluctuations and changes, which are always disagreeable and often hurtful."

The Scotch College at Paris had for some time, been a source of difficulty to the Bishops. They never had so much control of it as would have been most beneficial to the mission. For a long time, however, everything proceeded harmoniously, especially during the days when the Innes family were concerned with its management. They always deferred to the wishes of the Bishops; and the College became famous during the prefecture of Thomas Innes, so well known and eminent as an author and antiquary. The next generation of the Innes family were alike successful in maintaining a good understanding with the heads of the mission in Scotland. From its first institution the Paris

College had given valuable aid to the cause of religion in Scotland. It had produced many excellent missionary priests. Its doors were always open to fugitive missionaries, who were so often obliged, when life and liberty were threatened, to leave their country and seek safety abroad. Students on their way to Rome were always kindly entertained at Paris, and as a relief to the Scotch mission the expenses of the remaining part of their journey were defrayed by the superiors of the College at Paris. On their return, likewise, they were welcome guests, and often induced to prolong their stay at Paris until they learned anew their native language and acquired complete knowledge of their future duties. Moreover, the public funds of the college, as well as the private means of its heads, were, time and again, applied for the relief of the pecuniary distress of the mission. They also gave information concerning the difficulties of missionary priests in Scotland, to the early Scotch agents at Rome, who knew little or nothing about such things. They maintained a weekly correspondence with Rome, and apprised the agent there of the miseries of his native country, suggesting, at the same time, remedies and stimulating his zeal till they were applied. On the death of Mr. George Innes, in 1752, the last of the Innes family who had relations with the college, the harmony which had so long subsisted between it and the mission began to decline. The new Principal, Mr. John Gordon, of Achintoul, or Dorletters (hence his name often occurs in the correspondence as *Mr. Dorlet*), was less careful to secure the confidence of the Bishops in his administration. The dissatisfaction of the Bishops arose from the less perfect state of education. The defective training of the young ecclesiastics deprived the mission of many promising subjects; and it often happened that students, designed for the Church, returned home as laymen and even fell away from their religion. The Bishops remonstrated with the Principal, but to no purpose. On the death of Mr. Gordon, in 1777, hopes were entertained of improvement in the government of the college. His successor, Mr. Alexander Gordon, enjoyed a fair reputation in Scotland, having served the mission for many years, and who was, at the time of his appointment as principal, agent or procurator, for the clergy at Edinburgh. He took with him from Scotland, when he went in 1778, to enter on his charge of the college, two of the best students at Scalan. Such beginnings led to the hope that the college would soon renew its ancient reputation, and become, once more, a nursery of serviceable priests. This, however, was not its destiny. The two young men referred to returned home without completing their studies. This was a cause of grief and disappointment to the Bishops; and the revelations made by one of the students, who had returned, were far from affording them any comfort, and only caused further inquiry to be made. One of the two youths when suffering from a severe illness, which ended in his death, spoke his mind to Bishop Hay, personally, and by letter. He assured the Bishop that his loss of health and premature return home arose from the distress of mind caused him by the abuses that had found their way into the college, and to which he ascribed the defection of his fellow-student and others whom he named. Bishop Hay, when at Paris, on his way to Rome, in 1782, inquired more particularly into the management of the college than was to the liking of Mr. Gordon. The quarrelsome temper of the Principal was not unknown. He had given too good proof of it in the protracted dispute which he held with the Bishop concerning the maintenance of his insane brother.

The subject of the college and Bishop Hay's investigations came before the annual meeting at Scalan in 1783. Vacancies having occurred at the college, the Principal applied for subjects to fill them. Instead of at once complying with this request, the Bishop laid the case of the college before his colleagues.

He imparted to them the information which he had received from Mr. Peter Hay, the student, together with the confirmation of the same which he found by personal examination when at Paris. Considering the abuses which prevailed and the persistency of the Principal, he urged on them the extreme measure of declining to send any more boys until the college should be placed in a more satisfactory condition. The other Bishops were greatly swayed by his arguments; but dreading an open rupture, opposed so vigourous a resolution. Their opinion, however, did not prevail, and the Principal was, in due course, advised that he need expect no more students from Scotland until a complete change of system take place in the college. The well-founded fears of Bishops McDonald and Geddes were now realized. The Principal showed that he could retaliate. He met what he called the unjustifiable interference of the Bishops by suspending the funds in Paris belonging to the seminary at Scalan, pretending that their object was the maintenance of boys while preparing for the college at Paris. It appears that there were funds belonging to the mission in his hands, which, on similar grounds, he also sequestrated. The singular talent of Bishop Geddes for making peace was zealously employed but in vain; the Principal remained unmoved impervious to reason.

The authority of the Prior of the Carthusians over the college was superior to that of the Principal. To him, therefore, the Bishop appealed against Mr. Gordon's measure of retaliation. This appeal was written in French, and dated January 27th, 1784. The whole subject was treated therein with the Bishop's usual method and completeness. Some of his arguments may have been weak and defective, but his reasoning, on the whole, was sound and his cause just. The appeal was sent under cover to the Nuncio at Brussels, and along with it a request that the Nuncio at Paris would deliver it to the Prior with his own hand. This was done. The Prior, de Nonant, was wholly on the side of the Principal, and returned to the appeal a brief and supercilious reply, repeating and defending his determination to arrest the funds in Paris that belonged to the seminary, as long as the Scotch Bishops refused to send students to the college. The Bishops were not of a mind to recede from their position. "It is better," said Bishop Hay, "to send none (no students) there than to send and have them ruined." The Bishop ably rebutted the Prior's arguments, and insisted on the conclusion of his appeal. Bishop Geddes also, as procurator of the mission, wrote to Paris protesting against attaching the funds of the mission in a cause wholly foreign to their objects and destination. By his courteous manner and wonderful skill in negotiation, he prevailed so far as to effect a compromise in regard to the matter of funds, until the principal question at issue should be decided. The Principal himself was pleased to write a pamphlet, dated April 20, 1785, and had it edited in London by Dr. Alex. Geddes. It was read and discussed at great length in presence of the Bishops and administrators at their annual meeting of 1785. "It was such a paper," Bishop Hay stated, writing to Mr. Thomson, "as might be expected from such a source—full of misrepresentation, falsehood and acrimony." The Bishops at this meeting resolved on a proposal to the effect that if the Paris College wanted boys, it must choose them and pay for their board at Scalan, as well as for their outfit and travelling expenses on leaving it. The persistent Principal not only put his pamphlet in circulation through the London press, but also talked loudly of carrying the cause to Rome, unless the Bishop would retract his charges against himself and his college. The Bishop, in reply, said he was welcome to write to Rome, and that his opponent would willingly meet him there. Moreover, he would not refuse to retract or apologize for any misrepresentation which he might inadvertently have made, on his becoming aware of it; but he would never think of acknowledging the false interpretation that had been put upon his words.

The Bishop was now suffering in mind from the opposition and ill success which he had met with. The failure of his negociations regarding the Colleges at Paris and Rome gave him great concern. The resistance to his wishes at the annual meeting which had just been held; the dislike of some of the clergy to his episcopal rule, together with the abuse which they heaped upon him, weighed heavily on his mind. All this, with his ceaseless labour, caused depression of spirits, and to such a degree that he desired to resign his high and laborious charge. Nothing came of this, however. After considerable discussion with his coadjutor and other friends, who were all opposed to his resignation, the idea was abandoned, and the comparative ease which, the meeting and its cares being at an end, he enjoyed, favouring his health, he continued his labours with the usual zeal and energy; while the desire of resignation, once dismissed from his mind, these labours were persevered in for the long period of twenty years that still lay before him, and, with a degree of courage that no trial or hardship or anxiety could overcome.

In the autumn of this year, 1785, the restoration of the chapel on the east side of Blackfriars' Wynd, popularly known as "the Highland Chapel," was completed. The expense, considering the circumstances of the mission, was considerable. The pecuniary sacrifice, however, was not made in vain ; for, notwithstanding the unfavourable situation, the restored chapel was a source of great benefit to the Catholic community. It was looked upon, at the time, as one of the best chapels in the kingdom ; and it is noteworthy that it possessed a fine painting by an eminent artist, and that it was coeval with some of the structures that are still the pride of Edinburgh ; while marking the prosperity of that day, the new University was in prospect, and the " North New Town" had advanced westwards, almost opposite the castle.

It was now judged necessary that an answer should be given to Principal Gordon's "*Memoir*" regarding the College at Paris. It was, indeed, nothing better than a scurrilous libel—a series of misrepresentations and calumnies from beginning to end. Nevertheless, as it was sent under seal to every priest in both divisions of the mission, it was calculated to create an unfavourable impression unless a true statement of the whole case were prepared and placed in the hands of the clergy. The Bishop, accordingly, drew up a paper in the form of a letter addressed to his " Brethren of the Missions of Scotland," in which he gave a full and distinct account of everything connected with the affair of the college, accompanied by such vouchers for all he advanced as would stand the strictest examination. This paper when shown to the clergy produced the desired result. They were all satisfied as to the falsehood of the Principal's assertions, and so thoroughly disgusted with the insolence of his language as to render it unnecessary to do anything more in the matter. The compromise which Bishop Geddes had succeeded in effecting with the Principal regarding the Scalan and Deeside rents, was confirmed and made permanent, Mr. Gordon agreeing to continue the payment of them as a gift of his good will.

CAP. XXXVII.

GLASGOW—BAD SEASON—1786—AND DREAD OF FAMINE—HOUSE OF SCALAN IN DANGER—ANNUAL MEETING—THE BISHOPS' WRITE TO PROPAGANDA THAT ALEX'R. MCDONELL, A CANDIDATE FOR THE MITRE WHEN ALEX'R. MCDONALD WAS APPOINTED VICAR APOSTOLIC AND BISHOP OF POLEMO, EMIGRATED TO CANADA WITH 500 OF HIS CONGREGATION—THEY STATED ALSO THAT THE BISHOP OF POLEMO WAS RESIDING AT A SEMINARY ESTABLISHED AT SAMALAMAN, ON THE WEST COAST OF SCOTLAND—THEY ENDED BY EXPRESSING THE NEED THERE WAS OF MORE PRIESTS—THE EARL OF BUTE AND HIS BROTHER COMPLETE THE MONUMENT TO ABBATE GRANT—CONFIRMATIONS—PUBLICATION OF THE "PIOUS CHRISTIAN"—BISHOP HAY'S WORKS VERY POPULAR IN GREAT BRITAIN AND IRELAND—BISHOP GEDDES AND ROBERT BURNS—AN EXECUTION—GLASGOW MISSION—STUDENTS OF THE ROMAN COLLEGE—EFFECTIVE DISCIPLINE—MR. THOMSON WRITES MEMOIRS OF THE SCOTCH MISSION—BISHOP HAY'S "OPPOSITION"—CURIOUS DISCUSSION AS TO WHO WERE THE BEST CANDIDATES FOR THE PRIESTHOOD.

At this time the congregation at Glasgow was making favourable progress; and it met with all encouragement from Bishop Geddes, who took great interest in it, and favoured it with regular missionary priests' visits. He even expressed to Bishop Hay his confidence that, with proper management, a missionary priest might soon be placed there; but it must be one who knew the Erse or Gaelic language. The Bishop replied at once that it gave him great pleasure to hear such good accounts of matters at Glasgow, but regretted that a priest could not yet be found to supply that interesting mission.

This year, 1786, there was but too much reason to fear the calamity of famine. The early summer was ungenial, and there was ground for apprehending that the harvest would be as disastrous as those of 1782 and 1783. Another such season, Bishop Hay considered, and the country would be entirely ruined. Nor would this surprise him, wickedness having gone to such a height; and, indeed, he feared that it was daily increasing. His health improved as the summer advanced, and preparations were made for holding the annual meeting at Scalan. The house there narrowly escaped being destroyed the preceding April. A spark from a chimney had set fire to the thatched roof; and if the rising fire had not been observed in time, the whole house would have been consumed. Great efforts were made in pulling the thatch to pieces ; and so the fire was speedily subdued. The Bishops assembled as usual, and despatched to Rome their annual report on July 28th. They informed Cardinal Antonelli and Propoganda that Alexander MacDonell, a priest, who was a candidate for the mitre, when another Alex. MacDonald was appointed Vicar Apostolic of the Highland district, with the title of Bishop of Polemo, had emigrated to Canada with five hundred of his flock. They also stated that the Bishop of Polemo was residing in a seminary which had been established at Samalaman, on the west coast of Scotland. The Bishops concluded their report by expressing an earnest desire for more missionary priests in Scotland; thus showing that religion was progressing, and the field-for clerical labour widening from year to year. By September, Bishop Geddes was again at Edinburgh, and Bishop Hay at Aberdeen. Mr. Thomson, in a letter of this month, informed his friend, Bishop Hay, of the noticeable circumstance that John, Earl of Bute, and his brother, James Stewart Mackenzie, had completed the erection of a monument to their friend, the late Agent, Abbate Grant, in the church of the Scotch College at Rome. It consisted of a marble slab, with a medallion of the worthy agent and an appropriate inscription. The cost was about £50 sterling.

Bishop Geddes, soon after his return from the meeting at Scalan, undertook the visitation of the Galloway missions. He administered confirmation at several places. There were twenty-seven confirmed at Kirkconnel, now New Abbey parish; fifteen at Munshes, now replaced by Dalbeattie; and twenty-three at Terregles, now united with Dumfries. Any Catholics there may have been at Parton besides Mr. Glendonwyn, the proprietor, must have attended on occasion of the episcopal visitation at Munshes, as the Bishop did not visit Parton, having ample opportunity of meeting Mr. Glendonwyn at Dumfries.

Once more we have the pleasure, this year, 1786, to find Bishop Hay in the midst of his theological studies. The result was the publication of the "*Pious Christian*," which may be considered a continuation or third part of the "*Sincere*" and the "*Devout Christian*." When engaged in the preparation of this work, he derived much comfort and relief to the ailment in his side from the use of the Spanish *Foja*, which Bishop Geddes had provided for him. This improvement in his health was a cause of great joy to him as it facilitated so much the application to study that was necessary in completing a work of such importance. In March it was ready for the press, and the printer was set to work. Considering the state of the Bishop's finances, the expense was comparatively considerable. He accordingly sought the aid of subscriptions, and asked Bishop Geddes to order some copies. It was not intended to be an expensive volume. The price was to be half a crown (62 cents) or three shillings (75 cents). On the 21st of June it was reported complete. Its title is rather a long one—"*The Pious Christian Instructed in the Nature and Practice of those Exercises of Piety which are used in the Catholic Church.*" The Bishop himself thus describes it : "It is, therefore, an ascetical explication of the Manual, and as all the prayers of the Manual are added, after the explication, it is also a Manual itself." In the introduction, the Bishop still further explains his choice of title, "Having in *The Sincere Christian* instructed in the faith of Christ those who are seriously desirous to know the truth ; and having in *The Devout Christian* instructed those who are truly resolved to obey God in what his holy law requires from them in order to please Him, we now propose in the present work, to instruct the pious Christian in the nature of those holy exercises of piety which he practices, and in the manner of practicing them, so that they may be of real benefit to him, and effectually enable him to keep the commandments of God, to sanctify his own soul and secure his eternal salvation." An objection had been made to the method of examination of conscience, under a certain class of sins. The author, in writing to Bishop Geddes, thus replied : As to the objections against the examination in 6th, all I need say is that I made it my endeavour to have as little of the prayers, etc., of my own composing as I could, when I could get what was to my purpose in other English Manuals, especially in those which are generally most esteemed. Among these I always considered *The Garden of the Soul* as one of the standards, and the many editions it has gone through show the public approbation. I therefore thought I could not be better screened than in taking it for my guide ; and you will find the table of sins in *The Pious Christian* is just transcribed from *The Garden of the Soul*. You may hint this to the objector if you please.".... It would appear that the objection has been generally sustained, public sentiment sanctioning the principle which it involves. The more recent editions of *The Garden of the Soul* have adopted the proposed change, judiciously leaving the examination of conscience under the head referred to, to the suggestions of private inquiry. It is scarcely necessary to say that the instructive works of Bishop Hay were very popular among Catholics generally. In Ireland, especially, they were highly esteemed. Wogan, the Dublin printer, who had been charged with the Irish edition of the Bishop's earlier works, in writing to inform him of the death of the much regretted Archbishop Carpenter, took occasion to express his thanks for the great success that had attended the reprint of four volumes of the Bishop's works, and said, at the same time, that he hoped to enjoy his patronage in the future.

We seldom read in the history of our Bishops of their taking any concern in matters beyond the sphere of their ecclesiastical duties and occupations. Hence, it gives all the more pleasure to find the accomplished Bishop Geddes expressing his appreciation of a rising author who came, in due time, to be recognized as the Poet of Scotland. Genius only is the judge of genius; and we set down the words of no ordinary critic, when we record the opinion which Bishop Geddes entertained of the poetical ability of Robert Burns. The capital of Scotland was, at the time, 1787, a seat of literary taste and fashionable society. The Ayrshire Bard had just emerged from his rural privacy, and was a welcome guest in the brilliant circles of the time. Bishop Geddes, writing to Mr. Thomson, the agent of the mission at Rome, thus speaks of the youthful poet who was destined to become so celebrated: "One Burns, an Ayrshire ploughman, has lately appeared as a very good poet. One edition of his works has been sold very rapidly, and another by subscription, is in the press." Repeating the news to the same correspondent, the Bishop says: "There is an excellent poet started up in Aryshire, where he has been a ploughman. He has made many excellent poems in old Scotch, which are now in the press for the third time. I shall send them to you. His name is Burns. He is only twenty-eight years of age. He is in town just now ; and I supped with him at Lord Monboddo's, where I conversed a good deal with him, and think him a man of uncommon genius ; and he has, as yet, time, if he lives, to cultivate it." The good Bishop, moreover, showed his appreciation by taking an active interest in the young poet. In the subscription list prefixed to the Edinburgh edition of Burns' poems, published in 1787, are to be found the Scotch Colleges and Monasteries abroad, beginning with Valladolid, of which Bishop Geddes had been so long Principal. No other than the kindly Bishop could have caused them to be inserted. The poet was not ungrateful. He addressed a very interesting letter to the Bishop, in which is preserved the memory of this obliging act, as well as of the friendship that had arisen between the Bishop and the Bard. We learn also from the same letter that, at the time it was written, the Bishop's copy of the poems was in Burn's possession, for the purpose of having inserted some additional poems in the poet's own hand. It is also stated that Burns looked forward to the pleasure of meeting the

Bishop at Edinburgh in the course of the following month.

The good Bishop was not always so agreeably engaged as in conversing with poets and dining with the judges of the land. We find him as profitably and with more edification, imparting the consolations of religion to an unfortunate man, for whom there was no longer any earthly comfort. So recently as the days of Bishop Geddes, the extreme penalty of the law was inflicted on account of less crimes than murder, wilful fire-raising, etc. A young Irish soldier had become intoxicated, and, when in this state, got implicated in a robbery. For this crime, according to the practice of the time, he was under sentence of death. The Bishop himself discharged the painful duty of attending him to the scaffold. The ill-fated youth, it is related, behaved most becomingly.

In January of this year Bishop Geddes once more visited Glasgow. He not only found that the Catholics there were gaining ground, his congregation amounting to seventy members, but also—and which was of no small importance—that many leading people in the town showed no displeasure at the occasional meeting of the Catholics for public worship, although they had, for some time, been aware of such meeting. Several professors of the University availed themselves of the Bishop's visit to show him due civility. These were hopeful signs ; and the Bishop was encouraged by them to make arrangements with Mr. Alex. MacDonald, who was stationed at Drummond, to visit the Highlanders of Glasgow some time in the ensuing Lent. It can easily be conceived what pleasure it gave Bishop Hay to hear of so much progress where little or none had hitherto been hoped for. This was the first permanent missionary arrangement proposed for the capital of the West of Scotland ; and the Bishop wrote at once to impart his sanction. At the same time came an unpleasant communication from Cardinal Protector Albani, at Rome, complaining of some students whom the Bishops had sent to the Scotch College, and finding fault with the Bishops for sending such unfit subjects. It is by no means surprising, considering the defective discipline which prevailed in the College, that certain youths had not been successful. The state of the College must have been greatly to blame ; and such was the conviction of the Bishops. Bishop Hay was at first inclined to adopt measures similar to those which had ended in a rupture between the Bishops and the Paris College. But, judging from experience, he thought it was the part of prudence to yield to the opinion of his colleagues. Hence it was stipulated that, provided the arrears of Cardinal

Spinelli's legacy to Scalan were paid, and Mr. Thomson permitted still to reside in the College, the Bishops would be satisfied, and wait the dispositions of Providence, confidently hoping that in course of time an end would come to the ill-disciplined condition of the College.

The Bishop, with his usual consideration, received at this time into his house at Aberdeen, a youth whom Mr. Robertson recently appointed to the Buchan mission, highly recommended. This student he found to be deserving of all that had been said in his favour; and he proposed sending him to the College at Douai.

Mr. Thompson, meanwhile, in order to beguile the weary hours of his unpleasant position at Rome, which was attended with much vexation, employed his abilities in writing memoirs of the Scotch mission. He relied for information chiefly on letters and papers which had belonged to the late agent, and other documents. Many of these had gone astray; and many more had perished.

Bishop Hay's episcopal government like some civil governments of our time, appears to have had an *opposition ;* and it was not always a very loyal one. In the earlier days of the mission it was mostly the better class of society that supplied students for the Church. This better class consisted of the nobility and gentry, together with their tenant farmers of the higher order, who formerly intermarried with the lairds and nobles. The chief hope for a supply of ecclesiastical students, at the time of which there is question, depended on the lowest class of farmers, mostly those who laboured on their farms with their own hands. The Bishop insisted on availing himself of this source of ecclesiastical supply for renewing and perpetuating the priesthood. The *opposition*, and it had, as concerned this question the support of the coadjutor, strongly resisted this policy, if *policy* it may be called. Bishop Geddes and others argued for birth and family connection, as a condition of selection to the ecclesiastical state. Bishop Hay, in order to justify his way of proceeding, prepared a carefully written and elaborate document, in which he enumerated and discussed the objections that had been made to students whom he recommended. To the first objection—*inferior birth*—the Bishop thought it sufficient to reply that his predecessors had never considered it an obstacle to the admission of students, and that many of the humblest origin had turned out an ornament to the mission. *Infamy* of a student's near relations, although as an objection entitled to more consideration than the preceding, the Bishop demonstrated, both in theory and from former practice, to merit no more than a qualified regard; and he showed the injustice of universally rejecting a young man, otherwise promising, merely because some of his family had misconducted themselves. Neither was the circumstance of the candidate for admission, having formerly been engaged in service, considered by the Bishop as disqualifying him from aspiring to the priesthood. This opinion he supported by several precedents in the history of the mission. A final objection arose from the age of the candidate being considerably in advance of the usual period of life at which boys entered the seminary. The Bishop disposed of this difficulty as one having less pretentions to weight than any of the preceding. The good dispositions of a young man aspiring to the priesthood must be taken as a manifestation of the Divine will in regard to his vocation. In opposition to such proof none of the objections above stated ought to be allowed to weigh. These objections are not found among the *irregularities* which the Church enumerates as impediments against admission to the priesthood. These, the Bishop truly observes are all directly or indirectly personal to the candidate; and they are frequently dispensed with. It may, therefore, be safely concluded that it never was according to the mind of the Church that any of the circumstances objected to should disqualify for her service a person otherwise fitted for it.

CAP. XXXVIII.

DISCUSSION CONTINUED—THE ENGLISH CATHOLIC COMMITTEE—INNOVATION DREADED—ANNUAL MEETING OF 1787—INCREASE OF CHURCHES—MR. MATHIESON—DUNDEE MISSION—STATE OF SCALAN—MR. ANDREW DAWSON, RECTOR—BISHOP HAY'S RETURN TO EDINBURGH—SLOW TRAVELLING—THE PROGRESS OF RELIGION A GREAT PLEASURE TO THE BISHOP—ANXIETY CAUSED BY CONTINENTAL POLITICS—BISHOP GEDDES FOSTERS THE GLASGOW MISSION—"THE MERCHANT PRINCES" FRIENDLY—THRIVING INDUSTRIES—IRISH IMMIGRATION.

It is in order now to hear *opposition*. Its arguments, as urged by Bishop Geddes, may be summarised as follows: There was no great difference of opinion between the Bishops on general principles.

On two points only did Bishop Geddes insist on his own views. He held that persons of very humble origin were less fit to be selected for the priesthood, and surely his long experience, both at Scalan and Valladolid, gave great weight to his opinion.

There was much inequality in virtue and temper and ability in every rank of life; and Bishop Geddes had remarked that persons born in very low circumstances were liable to certain disadvantages which it was not easy to overcome; such as a littleness of mind, a timidity of temper, a vulgarity of sentiment and, too often, the grossness of vice. It was also a help to the success of a missionary priest that his family and near connections should be respected, and although objections on this ground might be counterbalanced by other considerations, a judicious superior ought unquestionably to take them into account in deciding as to the eligibility of a candidate for the ministry. We thus behold the man of humble origin, the son of a small and obscure farmer, arguing against the selection of candidates for the service of the Church, from the class to which he himself had belonged, whilst the man of ancient family and aristocratic connection vigourously supported the popular side of the question.

Bishop Hay appeard to think that considerable advantage belongs to the commencement of ecclesiastical training at the age of twenty and upwards.

Bishop Geddes, on the other hand, thought that such advantage is much diminished by increased difficulty experienced at that age, in undertaking a long course of study, and by the novelty of the mode of life. A special gift of perseverance and more than ordinary grace were necessary, he believed, to ensure the constancy of an adult candidate. It was manifest, both from reason and experience, that children and boys were trained to the observance' of exact discipline more easily than men whose habits of liberty had become formed, and who were naturally inclined to consider the exactness of seminary life unnecessary. "In this matter," said Bishop Geddes, addressing the senior Bishop, "you cannot judge solely from yourself. You had been accustomed to a studious life, and you may believe me, to the generality of grown up men, to be tied down every day, to some fixed task, appears a great confinement and a kind of slavery, especially if the first fervour should cool." Allusion was made to one or two points more in regard to which an adult student laboured under peculiar disadvantages, and then the learned Bishop concluded by stating, in his usual gentle style, that what he had said was not mere speculation, but the result of his own observation and of that of many others. Hence arose the desire of superiors of colleges in general to have young boys sent to them, whom they may train up in their own way. There are exceptions to what I have here said; but I think I have given the general rules, which I could illustrate with many examples, but it might be too long and otherwise inconvenient."

The Bishops were now engaged in the discharge of their episcopal duties, adding not unfrequently, parochial labours, when news reached them of certain proceedings of the English Catholics, which caused them much concern. At a general meeting in 1782, a committee, called "The Catholic Committee," had been appointed for five years, having for its object "to promote and attend to the affairs of the Roman Catholic body in England." This committee, when first constituted, consisted of Lords Stourton and Petre, Mr. Throckmorton, Mr. Stapleton and Mr. Thomas Hornyold. They seem to have limited themselves to the devising of a plan for the restoration of the hierarchy in England. But when they came to consult the four Bishops on the subject, they found such a variety of opinion, that the measure was dropped. As their power expired in 1787, a new committee was appointed at a general meeting of the English Catholics on the 3rd of May, in this year. It was then resolved that the regulations under which the former committee had acted should remain in force, and that the new committee should consist of ten members instead of five. Half their number were to be elected by the general meeting and the other five returned by the gentlemen of the four ecclesiastical districts and by those of Lancashire and Cheshire as a fifth ecclesiastical district. It was further resolved that they should meet annually on the first Thursday of May, and that Mr. Charles Butler should act as their secretary. Many of the clergy felt uneasy at the prospect of innovation which arose. Bishop Hay shared in this feeling, and applied to Bishop Talbot for information as to the proceedings decided on at the meeting. The Bishop replied, stating that, much against his will, he had been induced to attend the meeting; and that he had found the committee full of sanguine hopes for their projects, but openly declaring, at the same time, that nothing should be done without the concurrence of the clergy; and, indeed, nothing was determined on as regarded their future operations, and the whole question was postponed for a year. On receiving this reply, Bishop Hay concluded that nothing would ever be done if the intentions of the committee corresponded with their promise of acting in concert with the Bishops. Bishop Geddes, like his venerable colleague, and the rest of the clergy, was alarmed at the idea of innovations devised and introduced by unauthorized laymen. It was, indeed, no slight beginning of innovation that those decemvirs should take it upon themselves to regulate the affairs of the Church, even although they promised graciously to allow the clergy to concur with them. The learned Bishop evidently dreaded lest their action should result in schism. "I am alarmed as well as you," he wrote, "at the thoughts of innovations among our friends in England. I wish they may have a prudent agent at Rome. I wish there may not arise divisions at home.......Whatever comes' we must remain particularly attached to the centre of unity. This is surely the safest method for us." Bishop Hay also feared that evil would arise from the proceedings of the English Committee. "Who knows," he writes to the agent at Rome, "the influence of their intrigues or their plans?" The agitation at Rome regarding national colleges may have tended to originate this state of things. One result of this agitation was a scheme to establish, by general contribution, a school at home for the education of youth, the masters of which should be chosen by the contributors. Bishop Hay was apprehensive that the carrying out of this scheme would be attended, if not with absolute schism, at least with serious divisions, which would be highly detrimental to the cause of religion.

There does not appear to have been any business of great importance before the annual meeting of the Bishops, which was held this year, as usual, at Scalan. In the account of matters which they prepared for Propaganda, they could give a favourable view of the progress of religion. The spirit of persecution had greatly diminished, as was shown by the greater number and better style of churches which the Catholics were enabled to erect. Such important places as Huntley, Glenlivat, and Strathdown were now to possess churches, so steadily was the light of religion spreading from the private dwelling and the hidden chamber, to the more public places of the land, and edifices devoted to its celebrations, where all men could come and experience its consoling influences. The churches now built were not of a high style of architecture; but were solidly constructed and roofed with slate—not with humble thatch, as at a less prosperous epoch. Mr. Geo. Mathieson had, this year, enlarged the chapel at Tynet, adjoining the park of Gordon Castle, greatly adding to the commodiousness and beauty of the building, which his predecessor, Dr. Alex. Geddes, had begun. It may be mentioned, as indicative of the moderate spirit of the time, that the ducal family of Gordon, now Protestant, allowed the slates belonging to the deserted chapel of St. Ninian to be used by Mr. Mathieson for his new building. The Bishops congratulated themselves on the happy circumstance that churches were increasing "beyond what could have been dreamed of some time ago." (Bishop Hay.)

From this year we must date the commencement of the now flourishing mission of Dundee. It had, until the time referred to, been indebted to the priest of Stobhall for occasional assistance. When Stobhall was vacant, which not unfrequently was the case, it had recourse to Edinburgh, the Catholics of Dundee, still few in number, availing themselves of the good services of the Edinburgh clergy. The first resident priest was Mr. William Pepper, a religious of the Benedictine Order, from Wirtzburg, and who had been employed about a year as private tutor at Fetternear (Mr. Leslie's.)

Bishop Hay, after the meeting of the Bishops, prolonged his stay at Scalan during the whole of August in order to inquire into the affairs of the seminary. It had not been in a thriving condition under the management of Mr. Alex. Farquarson. On inspection the Bishop found everything in great confusion—many accounts remained unpaid; nearly all the provisions were exhausted, and the new building unfinished. His first measure was to call Mr. Andrew Dawson (grand uncle of the writer) from the Shenval mission, to take charge of the seminary, and to send the incompetent president to supply his place in the Cabrach. The incessant rains were an impediment to putting things in order out of doors. There was, however, no worse inconvenience than some delay. Only a sufficient supply of peats for one year had been carried in—a quantity deemed inadequate, it appears, by provident house-keepers. Within doors the Bishop gave great attention to the state of the books. They were all placed in order in the new part of the building. Those in ordinary use among the students were much worn, particularly Butler's Lives of the Saints, the English Bibles and Challoner's Meditations, all of which it was necessary to renew. The Bishop stayed a week more at the Seminary. Mr. Dawson willingly adopted his views of economical reform. In the second week of August, he hoped to be able to leave for the Enzie. The subject of Scalan occasioned great concern, both to the Bishop and his coadjutor. Nevertheless, they thought they saw the hand of Providence in all that had happened, as the means necessary and appointed for placing that house of ecclesiastical training on an efficient footing for the time to come. The expense incurred in reforming the Seminary caused the Bishop to contract considerable debt. Time only was wanting, however, for retrieving his financial condition. He enjoyed the satisfaction, meanwhile, to reflect that he had succeeded in clearing the Seminary of all its liabilities; and whatever he had sacrificed in so doing, he cheerfully presented to the institution. In addition, as increased "ways and means" to the Seminary, he was pleased to devote to it for a time the profits arising from the sale of his pills. So much for the material aid the Bishop afforded. At the same time he failed not to offer that moral assistance and encourgement which under the circumstances, were peculiarly valuable. This he did, chiefly through his coadjutor, begging of him to correspond with Mr. Dawson and encourage him in the fulfilment of his arduous duties. Mr. Dawson was necessarily dis-spirited by the sad state in which he found the Seminary. He had no reason, however, to despair. Bishop Hay had done much for the removal of difficulties; and now Bishop Geddes, by his friendly correspondence, helped greatly to reassure him and give him confidence. It was also a cause of satisfaction to him, as well as a support of his authority, that the senior Bishop laid down regulations, in writing, which indeed were nothing else than the discipline of the house as originally established. Advice from an instructor of youth of such large experience as Bishop Geddes was also of great value to him. The prelate who had been so successful at Valladolid recommended that the newly-appointed president should be much with the students, not only during school hours, but also at dinner and recreation time. He would be well repaid for this attention by the more rapid proficiency of the boys, and the personal comfort it would afford him when once he became accustomed to it. Bishop Hay wished, moreover, that he should be advised to attend particularly to his own religious affairs—meditation, spiritual reading, etc.

This year Bishop Hay revisited Edinburgh after an absence of six years from that Capital. He enjoyed there for a short time the society of his friend and coadjutor. He met also a gentleman, Mr. Heneage, who desired particularly to consult with him. His journey, according to the ideas of our time, was a tedious one. He travelled in a sort of stage coach, called "The Fly" (*lucus a non lucendo,*) probably because it did anything but fly. It took a day and a half from Aberdeen to Edinburgh, a distance which is now got over in six hours. It was no small pleasure to the good Bishop to witness THE PROGRESS RELIGION HAD MADE; the greater number of Catholics, their freedom from persecution, and the better state of their church accommodation. After twelve days' sojourn at the Capital, he returned, in improved health, to the north. On his return to Aberdeen he subscribed, together with some of his friends there, for *The Edinburgh Advertiser*, in order to see "how the threatening embroils on the continent might turn out." The political aspect was such that he was very much inclined to be of Pastorini's opinion. But he was confident that our Lord would prepare him and all our people for what might be coming, and "enable us to act our part so as to please Him."

It is highly interesting to note the pains which Bishop Geddes took with the infant mission of Glasgow. He little knew at the time what a giant he was so carefully nursing. In December of this year he spent ten days there in order the better to ascertain the wants of the small congregation and devise means of making some provision for them. One result was an arrangement with some of the chief people of the flock "to begin a little fund" for defraying the expenses of the priest who visited them from time to time. Not only did he ask nothing for himself, but also paid from his own resources the expenses of the visiting priest. He hoped that by summer the fund subscribed would amount to £20 (twenty pounds sterling). A society was formed for the purpose of forwarding the subscription; and a small house was to be leased in which the Catholics should meet on Sundays for prayers and spiritual reading, and where also the priest should lodge on occasion of his periodical visits. The zealous Bishop entertained the best hopes; and not without good grounds. The merchant princes of the western capital had shown friendly feeling; and the thriving industries of the place were already attracting that Irish immigration which was destined to increase so rapidly as to form, in a comparatively short time, about a sixth part of the entire population. The hopes of Bishop Geddes have been more than realized. It is only to be regretted that he did not live to enjoy the satisfaction of beholding at least a fair commencement of the great developments which have given to Glasgow so high a place in the Catholic world.

CAP. XXXIX.

EDUCATION—MR. ROBT. MENZIES—GÆLIC SERMONS—
ECCLESIASTICAL STUDENTS—BIGOTRY DECLINING,
1788—DEATH OF PRINCE CHARLES—NON-JURORS
PRAY FOR KING GEORGE—LARGE CHURCH AT PRES-
HOME—ANNUAL MEETING OF 1788 HELD AT GIBS-
TON—USUAL LETTER TO ROME—ILLNESS OF
PRESIDENT ANDREW DAWSON—BISHOP HAY PRESI-
DENT—FOUND SCALAN IMPROVED—DEATH OF
MR. CRUIKSHANKS—ORIGIN OF SCALAN—ITS
TRIALS—RECTORSHIP OF BISHOP HAY—BISHOP
GEDDES RETURNS TO EDINBURGH—IN BUCHAN—
AN OPINION OF BISHOP GEDDES—SUCCESS OF SCA-
LAN—CLIMATE THERE—SIGNS OF THE FRENCH
REVOLUTION—BERWICK WITHIN THE SCOTCH MIS-
SION.

At Edinburgh, meanwhile, the cause of education, which ought ever to go hand in hand with that of religion, was not neglected. Mr. Robert Menzies, the pastor of the Highland congregation, founded in the capital a school for poor Catholic children. He warmly appealed to Bishop Hay, pointing out the danger to faith and morals caused by so many poor children of his congregation being educated in Protestant schools. This consideration induced him to open a school in his chapel, where many poor children were taught reading, writing and catechism every day. A general class for catechism and religious instruction met on Saturdays in the forenoon. Two dozen children at first attended this class. As the attendance increased, thrice as many would be taught. Each pupil paid a small sum for tuition, Bishop Geddes undertaking to pay for six of the poorest of their number. In order that nothing might be wanting in the way of instruction for the Highlanders, Mr. Menzies delivered every Sunday afternoon a sermon in Gælic.

Bishop Hay, at the same time, took another boy into his house, who, together with John Ingram, was maintained at the Bishop's expense. As they were both promising subjects, it was hoped that they would become as serviceable to the mission as those who were sent to the colleges abroad.

A circumstance may be mentioned which shows that at this time the spirit of persecution was on the wane. Mr. Abernethy Drummond, so notorious as an enemy of the Bishops, addressed a polite note to "the Right Rev. Mr. Geddes," begging to know something of the character of a Mrs. Barclay, who, on leaving the Catholic Church, desired to join the non-juror sect of which Mr. Drummond was now the

Bishop. He also desired to learn the cause of her abandoning her Catholic friends. It further illustrates the better spirit of the time that Bishop Geddes visited with such distinguished Protestants as Dr. Webster, Mr. Maitland, and even Dr. Abernethy Drummond.

There now occurred at Rome the death of the Count of Albany (Prince Charles Edward). The news of his decease does not appear to have caused any sensation in Scotland. The Romans believed that the state of the British Catholics would be improved, political distinctions ceasing; and that there would be but one King and one people. This happy consummation had already taken place, when, some years before, Catholics in both divisions of the United Kingdom began to pray for King George. For a considerable time, indeed, the dynasty of the unfortunate Prince had been politically extinct. The non-jurors, even, in a synod at Aberdeen, held this year, resolved, at last, to pray for the reigning King of Great Britain.

The less perfect Church accommodation at Preshome came this year to be enlarged. The chapel at the Craigs was too small for the congregation; and the domestic chapel in the priest's home added nothing to their convenience. It was proposed, therefore, to build a strong and lasting edifice of stone and lime, with a slate roof, calculated to contain 700 persons. the need of money for this undertaking induced Mr. John Reid to be reconciled to the Bishop. The estimated expense was £350. The congregation chiefly was relied on for this amount ; and the people showed their good will by subscribing £100 within a fortnight. Some of the more wealthy promised to lend £100 more, until the congregation could repay them. In the choice of a site, it was desirable to avoid publicity by placing the building in a too conspicuous locality. Mr. Reid finally resolved to build in a part of his own garden, which, as the agents of the Duke of Gordon admitted, belonged to him. The baronet of Letterfourie and his brother took an active interest in the work ; and not only contributed very liberally, but also undertook to superintend the building. Their family arms were to be placed in front, and a fine monument of the two brothers erected within the church. In two months £330 were subscribed ; and on May 29th the foundation stone was laid by Letterfourie and his brother.

There was now question of the annual meeting and some anxious discussion as to the place where it should be held. The times were so much changed for the better, that it was no longer necessary to meet in a remote and secluded locality such as Scalan. Preshome was thought of ; and probably, but for the work which was proceeding there, the erection of the new church, would have been selected. Gibston, the residence of the priest near Huntly, was finally determined on as a suitable place for the Bishops and administrators to meet at, and from which to despatch their letters to Rome. At Gibston, accordingly, the Bishops and administrators met. The meeting was satisfactory; and the usual letters duly despatched to Rome. In their letter to the Cardinal, Prefect of Propaganda, they informed His Eminence that it had been resolved, in consequence of the illness of Mr. Dawson and the insufficient number of missionary priests, that Bishop Hay should act as president at Scalan, at least for a time. Mr. Dawson's illness was too serious to leave any hope of final recovery. He had been ailing all winter, and consumption was feared. As summer advanced his illness increased. Dr. Livingston was consulted, and found that consumption had made too fatal progress. He prescribed his immediate removal from Scalan, as, if anything could save him, it must be relief from anxiety and change of air. Bishop Hay, on his way to Scalan on the 1st of July, visited at a place called Brachlach, to see Mr. Dawson. He found him somewhat easier, but by no means out of danger. Even if he should recover, it would necessarily be a long time before he could resume his charge. The Bishop found that the change of masters had greatly benefitted the seminary. There was a considerable diminution of expense, so that a greater number of students could be maintained on the funds. The improvements which the Bishop had suggested were in course of being so well carried out that he was induced to say it gave him comfort amidst his other difficulties.

In May of the same year, Mr. Cruikshanks, who had been formerly chaplain at Traquair, and who had for some time been living retired at Edinburgh with Bishop Geddes, departed this life at the age of seventy-four. It is superfluous to say that so good a man was much lamented, not only by the Bishops and clergy, but also by all who knew him.

In the beginning of the eighteenth century great efforts were made by the Scotch Bishops in order to educate ecclesiastics, as well as other members of the Catholic community. It was a difficult task in face of the persistent persecution of that time. The schools which Bishop Nicholson and his coadjutor, Bishop Gordon, established, were situated in the more remote and least accessible districts of the Highlands. These were very useful for a time in preparing students for the foreign colleges and the general education of Catholic youth. At length, about the year 1712, the Bishops, availing themselves of the greater quiet which prevailed, and urged by the want of missionary priests, conceived the project of erecting a seminary in a less remote locality, where, in addition to the purposes which their schools had hitherto served, they might themselves train ecclesiastics and ordain priests for supplying the pressing wants of the mission. Aid was asked and obtained from abroad, and their plan was realized. A place, admirably suited to their purpose, was found in a retired part of the extensive lands of the Catholic Duke of Gordon. The chosen spot was far from any public thoroughfare, concealed from view by a circle of hills, and, at the time, partly surrounded by a morass—the only road to it a bridle path. It was just such a place as the Bishops had in view. Mr. William Reid, who was well acquainted with it, stated in 1778, that it was in as cold and stormy a region as there is in Scotland; and that the greater part of the provisions and things necessary for the house must be brought from a distance. But, as there was no security, as yet, against persecution, the very ruggedness and remoteness of the situation were its best recommendation. The infant seminary, besides, when so placed, could rely on the protection of the powerful house of Gordon, the chiefs of which had so long been vigourous supporters of the Catholic cause. On a not very lofty eminence, close to the left or western branch of a mountain stream, the Crombie, an affluent of the Livat, Bishop Gordon set down his seminary. There, in due time, he ordained priests; several who were educated there became distinguished—one in particular, who ever after bore the distinctive appellation, "Scalanensis." There also, Dr. Hugh MacDonald, so well known as the first Bishop of the Highland district, received his education.

In those evils day the remoteness of the situation did not always save the seminary from violence. The ministers of the Kirk renewed, from time to time, their hostility against the Catholic religion, disturbing its professors and directing their fury, in such ways as to inflict the greatest injury. In such circumstances, the seminary enjoyed no immunity. It was attacked several times by armed soldiers, who dispersed the community and shut up the house. Such was its hard lot in 1726; but, in the following year, the Bishops were enabled, through the influence of the Duke of Gordon, to re-open the seminary. In 1728 its occupants were again dispersed, twice over, in the short space of two months. On these occasions there was so little damage done, that soon afterwards, the establishment was once more occupied by its owners, and the usual course of study resumed. About the year 1738, Bishop Gordon considerably enlarged the building; and the superintendence was confided to Mr. William Duthie, a convert from Protestantism, who had studied at Paris, and also had been ordained there. In a month after the defeat at Culloden, a troop of soldiers burned the house to the ground, scarcely allowing the students and their masters time to escape to the hills, carrying with them their books and their altar furniture. Mr. Duthie, the president, was not, however, to be put down. He lived in a peasant's cottage until a place of shelter could be got ready for him at the site of the seminary. Such were his courage and spirit of perseverance, that he remained there till the year 1758, when his services being required at Edinburgh, he removed to that city. The seminary, as may be supposed, was in a very poor condition, and so remained until the Bishops who succeeded its founders, greatly feeling the want of such an institution, resolved on its restoration. The first step was the appointment of a competent rector; and such a one was found in the person of Mr. John Geddes, not long after his return from Rome. By his mental gifts he was peculiarly well qualified for the charge; but ill able, from the weakness of his constitution, to bear the fatigue and anxiety incident to the position. The place where the students lived, a mere hut, was not adapted for study. The indefatigable Mr.

Geddes, accordingly, lost no time in providing a commodious house on the opposite, or right bank of the river Crombie. To this house additions were made from time to time. The last of these was in progress when Bishop Hay assumed the office of President. Under the rule of Mr. Geddes, discipline, study and economy prevailed ; and so prosperous was the seminary that it had a greater number of ecclesiastical students ready to meet the demands of the foreign colleges than was required to supply them.

As has been shown, Bishop Hay undertook the charge of Scalan, when Mr. Dawson became so ill as to be unable to act. He was a very efficient President. He spent much of his time with the students, not only at the hours of study, but also in recreation time ; encouraging them in every possible way. His stay at the seminary was otherwise profitable. It afforded him the opportunity of learning from personal observation what outlay was necessary for securing its efficiency ; by retrenching all superfluous expenses, he laid down a sure and permanent basis for .economy in the future ; and by paying a handsome board for himself, he relieved the house from its pecuniary difficulties. Having occasion to spend a week at Aberdeen, he placed the work of the new building at Scalan, under the superintendence of Mr. Guthrie. He was much in want of a good altar piece for the new chapel there, and requested that his coadjutor would send to him an *Ecce Homo*, which Lady Chalmers had presented to him, and which had, for some time, adorned the altar "in the little closet of the back chapel in the old house, Blackfriars' Wynd." At the same time, he imparted to Bishop Geddes the mournful news that Mr. Andrew Dawson, the late rector of Scalan, departed this life on the 2nd of September, about 4 o'clock in the morning.

Bishop Geddes, after having been with his colleagues at Gibston, where the annual meeting was held, visited, on his way back to Edinburgh, his Catholic friends at Mortlach and in the Enzie, remaining in the latter place till the vigil of the Assumption. On that day, in the morning, he left Rannes, the seat of Mr. Andrew Hay, in company with the Rev. John Reid, partook of a fish dinner at the Earl of Findlater's and parted with Mr. Reid at Banff. From that town he proceeded partly on foot and partly on horseback, making a missionary tour through the destitute district of Buchan, saying Mass, preaching and hearing confessions at various places. In walking from the neighbourhood of Peterhead to Fetternear, he passed through Ellon, the birthplace of his old friend, Mr. Guthrie. The thought of his early friend, induced him to get a man to point out to him the house of Mr. Ross, the joiner, Mr. Guthrie's old master. He returned to Edinburgh, early in September, by way of Dundee and St. Andrew's. Once at home, he wrote to Bishop Hay, promising the *Ecce Homo*; and also informing the Bishop of some slight disturbance there was at Glasgow on occasion of Mr. McDonald's last visit. The same month Mr. Æneas Chisholm, afterwards Bishop in the Highlands, who had been for some time prefect of studies at Douai, passed through Edinburgh, on his way to Strathglass, to the mission of which he was appointed. It may not be of much importance to mention that he dined one day, together with Bishop Geddes, at the house of Mr. Arbuthnot, a Protestant gentleman, whose wife was a Catholic. But it is interesting, as showing the ideas that prevailed in regard to the two Bishops, to learn that the host took occasion to speak privately to the young priest, and offer him some good advice which might be useful to him. "There," said he, alluding to the two Bishops, "are two of the best men alive; but let me advise you to take Bishop Geddes for a model, rather than Bishop Hay. You know the severe things the latter has published about salvation out of your Church. I once spoke of them to Bishop Geddes, and hoped that he did not think the same way. He answered me only by saying, 'That is certainly the doctrine of our Church.'" Bishop Hay's plans for the improvement of the seminary had proved very successful. He was in high spirits, and wrote as follows to Bishop Geddes: "Who knows but Scalan may yet turn to be of good service in place of the college at Rome?......Our present subjects seem all very promising." The Bishop's health, too was all that could be desired; and, to complete his satisfaction, the harvest had been all secured much earlier than usual, a fortunate event which had not been witnessed since the year 1781.

Now were heard the first rumblings of the great political earthquake which was destined to overthrow the French monarchy and throw all Europe into confusion. Such was the anxiety of Principal Gordon, of the Scotch College at Paris, that so early as November in this year, he wrote, desiring to know how the Bishops of Scotland wished to dispose of the funds belonging to the mission, and at the time invested in French securities. Would they prefer to withdraw them at once, or await the results of the approaching meeting of the States general? Bishop Hay was inclined to leave the mission funds in Paris as long as the Principal, who must be the best judge, should think it unnecessary to withdraw the College funds. They should remain or be withdrawn together. (Dec. 12, 1788.)

In the beginning of January, 1789, Bishop Hay and his community were buried in snow and without the means of communicating with any other place. About the end of the month there came a thaw which raised the mountain streams to such a height as to cause as great an impediment to intercourse with the outer world as the snow had done. Letters had to wait whole days before they could be despatched. In a letter of 31st January, the Bishop expressed the gratification which the coadjutor's last report about Glasgow had given him, and hoped that their anticipations would meet with no "let." The winter did not end with the great thaw; and during the greater part of March, frost, wind and snow disputed with one another possession of the wild glen. The snow lay deeper and longer than at any previous period of the winter. At length, however, the state of the weather permitted the priests of the neighbourhood to reach the seminary on Holy Thursday (April 9,) although only a week before it seemed impossible that they should do so.

Among other places which Bishop Geddes visited was the town of Berwick, Bishop Gibson having admitted that it belonged to the Scotch mission. The Bishop prolonged his journey as far as York, in order to meet Mr. Douglas, the priest there, with whom he had become acquainted at Valladolid, when

Mr. Douglas was Prefect of the English College there. They travelled together to Stella Hall, and stayed a day or two with Bishop Gibson.

CAP. XL.

THE ENGLISH CATHOLIC COMMITTEE—MEMORIAL TO MR. PITT—DISABILITIES PARTIALLY REMOVED—PRESHOME CHURCH—BISHOP GEDDES ANXIOUS FOR GLASGOW — TOLERATION ADVANCING — BISHOP GEDDES AND ANTIQUARIAN RESEARCH—HIS CORRESPONDENCE WITH EMINENT MEN—DEPOPULATION OF THE HIGHLANDS—EDINBURGH GROWING—NEW SECRETARY OF PROPAGANDA—SEVERE WINTER—BISHOP HAY WILL NOT HAVE BERWICK IN THE MISSION---CONVERSIONS IN THE NORTH—A FRIENDLY PROTESTANT—MUSIC IN CHURCHES—AN INSUPERABLE OBJECTION—SEMINARY AT SAMALAMAN ENLARGED—CONVERSIONS—REV. DONALD CARMICHAEL—BISHOPS AT FORMAL MEETING DECLINE SENDING STUDENTS TO ROME—SCALAN PROSPEROUS —BOOKS FROM ROME—FEAR OF A BAD SEASON.

The "Catholic Committee" of England was once more at work, laudably engaged in endeavouring to obtain the repeal of the remaining penal laws. They had presented in February, 1788, a memorial on the subject to Mr. Pitt. That minister gave a favourable reply. There were, however, certain technical difficulties, and he recommended that they should delay their application to Parliament till the following session, and requested that, in the meantime, they should provide him with authentic evidence of the opinion held by the Catholic clergy and the universities with respect to the existence or the extent of the power, alleged to belong to the Pope, of dispensing subjects from their oath of allegiance to their Sovereign. Hence the application that became so famous, to the Catholic universities of the Sorbonne, of Louvain, Douai, Alcala and Salamanca, for an opinion on the subject. Both the minister and the committee were satisfied with the replies, and on the 19th of April, 1788, it was resolved to prepare a bill for the desired repeal. This work was confided to Mr. Butler; and if the committee could have had the bill framed as they originally designed, it would have placed the Catholics in the position of dissenters generally, without an oath of any kind. It may be mentioned, as showing that the committee was not entirely under lay influence, that in May, 1788, Bishop James Talbot, Bishop Berington, coadjutor in the Midland district, and Mr. Thomas Wilks, O. S. B., were added to its members. The distrust experienced by the clergy, as to the ulterior purposes of the committee, appears now to have passed away Bishop Hay considered that, as an effort was made to relieve the English Catholics of their disabilities, something might be done, at the same time, for Scotland; and he suggested to his coadjutor that some friendly person might be induced to use his influence in favour of the Scotch Catholics. Could not Bishop Geddes prevail on his friend, Mr. Henry Dundas, to interest himself in the cause and undertake to promote some measure of relief, either himself, or through some of his powerful friends?

Some hindrance was caused by the action of Lord Stanhope, who had charge of a bill in favour of certain classes of non-conformists, but who was not unfriendly to the Catholics. He recommended that the committee should adopt a form of protestation which he framed, disclaiming certain opinions which were falsely ascribed to the Catholics. The committee considered the protestation; and, from deference to the opinions of Bishops Thomas and James Talbot, made some alterations, when it was accepted. All the Bishops and nearly all the Catholic gentry and clergy in England affixed their signatures to it. A copy of it, together with a petition for the repeal of the obnoxious laws, was then laid before Parliament. In addition, the minister demanded an oath; and the committee was asked for a form which would meet the views of the Catholics. A form of oath, accordingly, was prepared, which, it was thought, would prove acceptable, as it was only an echo of the protestation, to which the whole Catholic body had formally assented. The ministry introduced an alteration to which the clerical members of the committee made no objection. Bishop Hay expressed strong dislike both to the oath and the protestation. This feeling was intensified by the exaggerated impression which the Bishop had received from the Aberdeen' newspapers, through which only he was, as yet, acquainted with the matter. All the Bishops of England, meanwhile, had signed the protestation, and two of them, who were members of the committee, gave their sanction to the proposed form of oath. The opinion of the oath throughout England was, however, quite in accordance with that of the Scotch Bishop. There does not appear to have been anything positively unorthodox in the oath or the protestation. But the language was coarse and unpalatable to Catholics. Bishop Geddes, in writing to Bishop Gibson, said "the oath was very exceptionable." In a letter to Mr. Thompson he wrote that much of the opposition to it was provoked by the designation of "*Protesting Catholic Dissenters*," which was inserted in it and in the proposed bill. For his part he would always call himself a *Catholi*, or, if there must be an addition, let it be only *Roman* or some such honourable word. Bishop Hay entertained a still less favourable opinion. He considered the oath an equivalent to the Oath of Supremacy. It does not appear, however, that it was so interpreted by the English Bishops, however much they may have disliked it. This feeling was so decided that they issued a circular letter addressed to their people condemning the oath, and forbidding Catholics to take it. Government, at length, was moved to modify the offensive expressions in the oath. Bishop Thomas Talbot alone was inclined to accept the oath as amended. Dr. John Douglas, who had succeeded Bishop James Talbot as Bishop in London, together with his two colleagues, gave no countenance to the amended oath and published a circular letter, similar to the former one, forbidding it to the Catholics in their districts. The Catholic Committee, wearied and distracted by so much variety of opinion, made no further attempt to alter the oath. The House of Commons, more friendly at the time to Catholics, passed the bill and oath without a dissenting voice. In the House of Lords, the Bishops had sufficient influence to cause the oath to be amended so as to meet their views. The English Relief Bill now became law. This is the more extraordinary as some ten years later it was found to be impossible to remove the remaining disabilities, notwithstanding the good will and the powerful efforts of Mr. Pitt. The obstinacy of George III. was unconquerable.

There now arose some difficulty at Preshome, so well known for a long time as the chief seat of the Catholic religion in the North. The new church had cost double what Mr. Reid had calculated on. The zealous priest was not, however, discouraged. *Illi robur et æs triplex circa pectus erat.* And his numerous congregation, which had at first contributed so liberally, was well able and not unwilling to assist him.

About the same time there was considerable anxiety on account of the mission at Glasgow, as yet in its beginnings. This arose from a threatening and anonymous letter which claimed to convey the determination of a body of men combined for repressing the growth of Catholicity. The magistrates of the city assured Bishop Geddes that the annoying letter was the work of a malicious person, and not of a combination. This, on mature enquiry, the Bishop found to be the case. Bishop Hay was not surprised at the anxiety of his colleague. Knowing, as he did so well, the character of the people, he dreaded lest the letter might be the prelude to something worse When, however, the facts were discovered, he expressed his satisfaction that there had resulted no evil consequence; the circumstance having only shown that the dangerous spark, which might be so easily fanned into a flame, was still alive among "that poor fanatical people." The age was advancing, and it would have required many sparks to stifle the spirit of toleration that was fast gaining ground.

The great care which Bishop Geddes bestowed on Glasgow and the other missions, did not prevent him from finding leisure for much correspondence on matters of antiquarian interest, on taste and literature.

Among his papers of this time are found letters from Principal Robertson, George Chalmers, author of "Caledonia," General Hutton, Dr. John Gregory, Sir William Forbes, Sir Alexander Livingston, the Duke of Montague and the Earl of Buchan. These letters from Protestant noblemen and gentlemen, most of whom were eminent literary characters, abound in courtesy, and are full of expressions of personal regard.

Writing to Mr. Thompson, April 18, the good Bishop expresses his regret that the Highland missions were likely to suffer from the depopulation of large tracts of country, to make way for sheep farms, whilst on the other hand, it was cheering to observe that Edinburgh was increasing. It was gradually advancing westwards. Hanover street, Frederick street, and even Castle street were formed. That fine building, the Register House, was completed, St. James' Square built, and the enlargement of Leith harbour begun.

Mgr. Borgia, who, as Secretary of Propaganda, had shown much friendship to the Scotch mission, was now elevated to the Cardinalate; the Bishops hoped, however, that his successor in the secretaryship would prove as friendly as His Eminence had always been. On occasion of sending a letter of congratulation to the new Cardinal, the Bishop imparted to the agent his views regarding Scalan. He had found the seminary in a state of confusion both within doors and without, and need of reform in its management. His expense in putting everything in order had been considerable. He regretted it not, however, as by the end of summer he hoped to complete his labours, and thus cause the seminary to be of more benefit to the mission than it had hitherto been. The winter had been unusually severe, but, nevertheless he enjoyed excellent health. Some additional expense was incurred by sending for letters to Keith or Huntley. But this was made up for by the diminishing of his cost for board, which was much less than when resident in a town. His only regret at the time was that nothing could be done towards improving the condition of the Scotch College at Rome. Bishop Geddes now wrote to compliment him on the recurrence of the anniversary of his consecration. Bishop Hay, in acknowledging the compliment, took occasion to write that whatever

Bishop Gibson might say about Berwick, it had never formerly been considered as part of the Scotch Lowland district ; and it appeared to him ridiculous that when there were two English churchmen within ten or twelve miles of it, you should be troubled with journeying thither. He never could and never would agree to such an arrangement. It was unreasonable, he insisted, that Bishop Geddes should take new and unnecessary burdens upon himself when they could not manage to fulfil their essential duties in what certainly belonged to them. The more pleasing news came from Bishop Geddes that bank dividends were continuing at eight per cent. It was still more gratifying to learn that conversions were occurring in the cold north. Two ladies of Orkney, a Mrs. Trail and her sister, Miss Chapman, had just been received into the Church, Mr. Trail fully consenting. Mrs. Trail was not destined to be the last convert of the name. Our age has been edified by the conversion of another lady of the name of Trail, who was long known as Sister Agnes Xavier. As further proof of the good understanding which now prevailed between Catholics and well-informed Protestants, it may be mentioned that when the Bishop had occasion to visit Lady Livingstone at Westquarter, who was a Catholic, her husband, Sir Alexander, although he was a Protestant, showed himself very friendly, and always sent his carriage to convey the Bishop a stage on his way to Glasgow.

A new subject of discussion arose from a very general desire among the congregations to have singing at the public services. Bishop Geddes and many of the clergy favoured this desire. It was, however, vigourously opposed by Bishop Hay, whose vivid recollection of former riots inspired him with the fear of fresh disturbances which the practice might occasion. Mr. Mathieson, who was missionary apostolic in the parish of Bellie, and who was an amateur musical instrument maker of distinguished ability, addressed to Bishop Geddes a long, eloquent and most ingenious pleading for the introduction of music into the Catholic churches. In his paper on the subject he fully discussed the merits of the case, as it was to be considered at the approaching meeting of the Bishops. Edinburgh had already made trial of music, as had also Mr. Mathieson's small chapel at Tynet, into which he had introduced it with the consent of Bishop Geddes. It could not, of course, be generally adopted without the sanction of the Bishop. The experiment at Tynet had cost much labour and expense. But not in vain. The result was larger congregations at Christian doctrine on Sunday afternoons. The chapel was also better attended on holydays than ever before ; he might say it was crowded. The people generally were edified, although, as was to be supposed, some objected to the innovation. As to exciting the jealousy of Protestants and occasioning unpleasant proceedings on their part, it only caused them to express surprise that Catholics had so long neglected congregational singing. Mr. Mathieson had made sure of their distinct approbation by wisely consulting several of various denominations. It was objected that the music was not well performed. The better attendance showed, if not that the music was excellent, that the congregation was well pleased with it. As to its excellence or inferiority, opinion would be formed according to taste and judgment. It would not be difficult, Mr. Mathieson conceived, to have as good music as their Presbyterian neighbours of the Church of Scotland. He was sustained by leading members of the clergy. Mr. James Robertson, now settled at Edinburgh, assured Bishop Geddes that his opinion was more and more confirmed that the introduction of music into the larger congregations was both practicable and desirable. Mr. John Gordon, missionary apostolic at Aberdeen, addressed his uncle, Bishop Geddes, to the same effect. It is difficult to understand how there could be *High Mass*, or even a *Missa cantata*, without singing. The use of any other music than that which belongs to such Masses, is certainly questionable. It does not seem reasonable that there should be chanting by the choir or the congregation during those parts of the Mass which the priest is directed to read or chant aloud, the *Gloria, Preface, Credo*, etc. At afternoon services, when vespers cannot be chanted, any devotional singing or music may be edifyingly introduced. None knew all this better than Bishop Hay. And, indeed, he expressed in the strongest terms the pleasure it would give him to see music introduced into their churches, if circumstances were such as to render it advisable. He promised even to encourage it, if it could be conducted with propriety and decency.

Bishop MacDonald was unable this year from an accident by which his leg was injured, to attend the meeting at Scalan. He was engaged at the time in enlarging his seminary at Samalaman, in the West Highlands. Bishop Hay and his coadjutor were the only Bishops present when the usual report was despatched to Rome. Bishop Geddes, on his way to Scalan visited Stobhall, and confirmed there, among others, a substantial farmer from Stormont, named Carmichael, a convert, together with his wife, his four sons and his two daughters. One of the sons was the late Donald Carmichael, many years procurator at St. Mary's College, Blairs, and who died a few years ago at an advanced age, when in charge of the mission at Peterhead. It was resolved at the meeting to continue to decline sending students to the Scotch College at Rome until some security should be given for reform in that institution. Scalan promised well ; and it could be none the worse for the Bishop's resolution to spend the next five years there, provided there occurred nothing to prevent him. No young priest could be expected from Scalan for three years ; and about the same time, before any of its subjects would be called for by a foreign college. The Bishop hoped in the meantime to advance the studies of some of them beyond what was usually attained by boys destined only for a short residence in the seminary. For this purpose he commissioned Mr. Thompson to purchase and send to him some necessary books ; such as *De chronia de arte Rhetorica*, *Cicero's Epistles*, *Minelli's*, if possible *Sterghenan's Instituta logicæ et Metaphysicæ*, and any other suitable work in Latin, history or philosophy. Cardinal Antonelli, also, would perhaps send him some from Propaganda. The summer in the country around Scalan had been very rainy. Unless improvement came soon very little grain would ripen, and there would be no peats, on which kind of fuel the people in those parts were very dependent. The rising of the barometer, however, afforded good hopes. The Crombie, in consequence of the heavy rains, rose higher in a few hours than was remembered by any one in the locality. At Banff, Keith and Elgin there had been terrific storms of thunder and rain, together with loss of life in some cases. At Scalan thunder was heard beyond the hills, but none in the vicinity.

CAP. XLI.

ANXIETY CAUSED BY THE FRENCH REVOLUTION—INCENDIARY FIRE AT STOBHALL—ORDER AGAINST MUSIC IN CHURCHES ENFORCED—ADESTE FIDELES—INSANITY—HIGHER STUDIES AT SCALAN—DEATH OF THE DUCHESS OF ALBANY—FIRST UNITED STATES OF AMERICA BISHOP—PROHIBITION OF MUSIC RELUCUTANTLY OBEYED—A CATHOLIC SOCIETY—VISITING THE MISSIONARY PRIESTS—DANGER OF MUSIC IN CHURCHES AROUSING LATENT HOSTILITY—EDUCATION OF THE POOR—LIBERALITY OF THE MAGISTRATES ON OCCASION OF AN EXECUTION—CARDINAL ALBANI MORE FRIENDLY—NO APPROVAL BY BISHOP GEDDES OF DR. A. GEDDES' SCRIPTURES—BISHOP GEDDES MISREPRESENTED.

Mr. Thomson, writing to Bishop Geddes, augured the worst consequences from the incipient revolution in France. Many eminent statesmen and patriots in England, meanwhile, were exulting over the fall of the Bastile and the extinction of despotism. Mr. Thomson showed himself more penetrating by his sinister predictions than Edmund Burke, who could not see the extent of the tragedy and overthrow that were in progress, until the forced return from

Versailles to Paris, of the unfortunate king, in the hands of the Parisian populace. Bishop Geddes, on his return from the meeting, visited his old friends in the Enzie. He found the new Church at Preshome well advanced. The slaters were busy roofing it. The Earl of Findlater had presented a fine painting of Gregory the Great, a masterpiece of one of the Caracci.

From the 18th to the 19th of August an incendiary fire occurred at Stobhall. The priest's servant and another man having been awakened by the smoke, gave the alarm and called Mr. Macpherson. Some of the neighbours cheerfully gave their assistance in extinguishing the flames ; others stood by or passed on unconcerned. But for the calm weather the whole premises must have been consumed. As it was, the fire was subdued, whilst only the thatch on one side of the chapel was destroyed. The fire having been willfully raised, and so many of the neighbours declining to aid in extinguishing it, there could be no doubt that the evil spark was still alive, and that the greatest caution was necessary to avoid any step that might fan it into a flame. On this account Bishop Hay considered that they were justified in the joint resolution which they had taken of putting a stop to the singing scheme, and he entreated his coadjutor to see it acted on without delay wherever singing was found to be in use. The Bishops at their recent meeting had concluded against singing in the churches. It was not, however, easily put down. Mr. Robertson informed Bishop Geddes that the orders relative to music had been received with all due submission, but that it was impossible all at once to get rid of their teacher. His friend, Mr. Menzies, on the other side of the street, had some hopes that the order against music would be recalled. He had none. But as it had been confided to the prudence of each missionary priest, he intended to let it dwindle away gradually, rather than stop it suddenly. It is said to be due to Mr. Menzies and his Highland congregation that the popular Christmas hymn, *Adeste Fideles*, was introduced into Scotland. It rapidly became the fashion in the city; apprentice boys whistled it in every street. It was even said that the black birds in the squares joined in the chorus. It is not a little remarkable that this Catholic hymn is now to be found in almost every collection of Presbyterian Church music, under the name of the *Portuguese hymn*.

Mr. Thomson feared lest the severe climate of Scalan should prove injurious to his friend, Bishop Hay. "Bishop Gordon, indeed," he wrote, "resided there frequently, during the latter days of his life, but only to retire from the hurry of business and enjoy a little respite from his apostolic labours. He chose that place because he had been the founder of it, always had a particular attachment to it, and treated it with peculiar favour." It was by no means certain that it would prove equally favourable to the health of Bishop Hay. A friend at Rome had requested the agent there to ascertain what books or other things the Bishop would like to have for his own private use, in order that this good friend, known to have been a Mr. Waters, might have the pleasure of sending them to him.

There were but few cases of insanity among the clergy. That of Mr. Gordon, brother of the principal at Paris, has been already alluded to. Another melancholy instance occurred in the person of Mr. James Cameron. This priest's mind became so affected that he wandered about the country for several months. It was finally arranged that he should reside with Mr. Macpherson at Stobhall.

If one may judge from a list of books at Scalan, a higher class of studies was now pursued there, under the auspices of its episcopal president. The books referred to which were sent from Edinburgh, were, among others, Altieri's Italian and English dictionary, Schrevilius' Lexicon, Eachard's classical dictionary, Knoxes' history of Scotland; two copies of a translation of the Mass, lately made by Mr. Robertson, priest at Edinburgh, and Buchan's medicine, a new edition of which was soon to appear, when it also would be sent. Besides these books, there was a Gunter's scale, a terrestrial globe and a ring dial, or astronomical ring of Bishop Geddes' own manufacture, and which he took pains to describe as designed for the old style. A set of purple vestments was also sent at the same time. Bishop Geddes, on occasion of sending these things, informed his right rev. friend, that a form of faculties which he had been preparing, was not yet printed. He asked the Bishop whether he would recommend that their form should be limited "till they are recalled," or to a certain number of years, say two or three? He was himself in favour of the former way. He could not conclude his letter without entreating the Bishop, and it was not till after serious consideration of the matter, to permit the singing of some hymns at Edinburgh and Aberdeen, on Sunday afternoons.

In a letter of 28th Nov., 1789, Mr. Thomson, informed Bishop Geddes of the death of the Duchess of Albany at Bologna, on the 17th Nov., 1789. The agent states in his letter that "she died in an edifying manner, and was much regretted." She left the Cardinal, Duke of York, her heir. There is also in Mr. Thomson's news the nomination of the first American Catholic Bishop of Baltimore, in the person of Mr. Carryl (Carroll.) He was mistaken, however, in stating that the United States had refused to receive a Vicar Apostolic with the title of Bishop *in partibus*. On the contrary, they declined all interference in the matter.

It would appear that Bishop Geddes concurred reluctantly in the peremptory prohibition of music which Bishop Hay had issued. He now according to promise, prepared his reasons for requesting that the prohibition should be so far modified as to admit of some hymns being sung in the churches of Edinburgh and Aberdeen, after Christian doctrine on Sunday afternoons. Great advantage, he insisted, would accrue to religion from the use of suitable music; and such had been sanctioned by the Church in every age. Music was mentioned by St. Justin, as part of divine worship, even at a time when the Christians were obliged to assemble in the catacombs. As to danger, from all that Bishop Geddes could observe, there was not the slightest fear of anything arising in consequence of the use of music in the churches. The great majority of the Catholics wished it, and they could not be made to understand why the Bishop should not encourage the practice. The prohibition was obeyed prudently and by degrees. But for this wise moderation, there certainly would have been scandal. The Bishop gave great weight to the following consideration : Sunday afternoons and evenings were times of peculiar danger to young persons. It was, therefore, a matter of great importance to attract them to chapel to Christian doctrine and devotion. In forwarding this desirable object, music would be a powerful influence. Its practice would also be a distant preparation for having High Mass sung on some festivals, which will tend greatly to the edification of the faithful when it shall be found to be expedient. "Your predecessor," he concludes, "was very desirous of seeing this ; and what he said to me on the subject was one of the reasons which I had for causing Church music to be taught at Valladolid. I wish the same were done in all our houses abroad. I beg you will consider all this; and I hope you will give a favourable answer to our petition. You shall hear of and see the good effects of it."

Catholics could now associate, and in the most public manner, for mutual benefit. So early as 1785 a burial society called "St. Andrew's Catholic society" was formed in the congregations of Edinburgh. It was so far successful that in November, 1789, its statutes, laws and regulations were made public in order to attract attention to it, and, in consequence, rendered it more efficient. Only Catholics of good moral character and sound constitution and whose age was not over thirty-six years could be admitted as members. A member, after five years of membership, was entitled to receive five shillings weekly, in the event of his becoming indigent. The expense of funerals was provided for from the funds of the society. The society was managed by a president, six directors, a treasurer and a clerk, who were elected annually. There were also three arbiters for settling such disputes as might arise between members. From their decision no appeal was permitted to any court of law. Parties who gave donations became honorary members. This society continued in full operation for many years. It was finally wound up, from thirty to forty years ago, and its capital divided among the members.

As appearances indicated severe weather at Scalan, it was thought best to appoint that the holy oils should be blessed at Edinburgh.

The Bishops were agreed as to the advantage of their visiting each missionary priest once in the year. This, however, although desirable, could not be done. The small number of priests rendered it necessary that the Bishops themselves should often attend to parochial duties. Hence, considering also their episcopal functions throughout each district, it was impossible for them to visit the clergy frequently, or reside with them any length of time. Their presence, therefore, must be dispensed with except in cases of business which could not be transacted by letter.

This year, 1790, the Bishop, notwithstanding the representations of Bishop Geddes, still held to his determination of prohibiting music in the churches. He had a more lively sense than his coadjutor of the lurking danger which existed. In some places, no doubt, Mr. Mathieson's mission, for instance, which was under the powerful wing of the Dukes of Gordon, any amount of music and singing would have been perfectly safe. But it would not have been so throughout the missions generally, where much less than a musical celebration of Catholic worship might, at any moment, have roused to activity the latent spark which was far from being extinguished. It was still alive, indeed, at a much later epoch, when the spirit of the age condemned it to inactivity.

The question of music being, for the time, disposed of, the Bishop gave his attention to another subject of great importance, the proper education of the children of the poorer classes. A Mr. Fleming kept a charity school near Scalan, at a place called Badevochla, causing such of the children to pay as he thought were able to do so. He obliged them to learn his Protestant catechism on Saturdays, threatening to expel all who refused. Mr. James Carruthers, the priest of the place, could not fail to see the injury that was thus done to the children of his congregation. Their heads were filled with erroneous ideas, the very opposite of what their parents and pastor taught them. They also became confused in their minds and were prevented from learning their own catechism, their time being given to Mr. Fleming's. Mr. Carruthers found a remedy. He brought from Galloway a young man, a native of Ireland, who had come to Scotland with a view of obtaining a situation as school master. His qualifications appear to have been superior to those of Mr. Fleming. He could teach reading, writing and arithmetic. He was, besides, a good Latin scholar, and was superior to Mr. Fleming as a penman. The people were much pleased, procured for him a school room and sent their children to him, preferring to pay a teacher who could instruct their children according to their own principles. Mr. Fleming and his friends, as may be supposed, were much offended and threatend to memorialize the society at Edinburgh for propagating Christian knowledge. As a Catholic school master was still proscribed by law in Scotland, Bishop Hay, apprehending evil results from the memorial and the misrepresentation and exaggeration which would probably accompany it, requested his friend and coadjutor to use his influence with a gentleman who was a member of the Propagation

Society in order to counteract the bad effects of the Fleming appeal.

The delicate position in which the Catholics and clergy, and even the higher magistrates stood, at this time, is well illustrated by the circumstances of a capital execution. The town council resolved to permit any Catholic clergyman to assist the culprit publicly on the scaffold. The Lord Advocate, on being consulted, declared that he saw, in this no impropriety. Bailie (alderman) John Hutton, a friend and former school-fellow of Bishop Hay, communicated the resolution of the magistrates to Bishop Geddes. The Bishop, however, dreading lest some of the rabble should raise a noise, declined the kindly meant offer with thanks, considering it sufficient to attend the unfortunate man to the last moment, in prison, and to be stationed during the execution, in a window close at hand; and so it was done. The magistrates invited the Bishop to dine with them after the dread ceremony. He could not but decline the invitation, whilst acknowledging their politeness. It would have been very unpleasant for him, on such an occasion, to accept, and would, besides, have made choice news for the populace. Bailie Hutton and Mr. Donaldson desired to be most kindly remembered to their old school-fellow, Bishop Hay. So also did his highly esteemed friend, Dr. Alexander Wood.

A change, at this time, came over the mind of Cardinal Albani, and he showed an inclination to be more friendly to the Scotch College. In view of the prospect which this better feeling afforded, Bishop Hay wrote to congratulate Mr. Thompson. It would appear that Bishop Geddes had given offence to some of their English friends by showing friendship to Dr. Alexander Geddes, and by so doing had injured himself and the Scotch mission. Bishop Hay remarked this in his correspondence with Mr. Thompson, and stated that he had remonstrated with his coadjutor. It is not, however, said that Bishop Geddes expressed any approval of Dr. A. Geddes' erroneous comments accompanying his translation of the Scriptures. He countenanced him as a distinguished man of letters, whilst, by breaking with him, he would have destroyed the best hope there was of the erring writer's reconciliation.

The great popularity of Bishop Geddes did not save him from misrepresentation. Some busy bodies among the Catholics of Edinburgh were pleased to circulate the rumour that Bishop Geddes, contrary to the prohibition which he and Bishop Hay had issued, allowed singing to take place openly in the Bishop's chapel; that a new teacher of music had been engaged at a salary of £35 a year; and that Bishop Hay was blamed for refusing a similar permission to Mr.

Menzies, on the other side of the street, a partiality which seemed to favour Bishop Geddes' chapel, on account of the rich people who frequented it. Bishop Hay, not knowing what to think of this rumour, wrote to his coadjutor for information. The latter, in his reply, remonstrated in the most spirited manner against such unfounded accusations. He writes at some length. It would be superfluous, however, to quote more than a few words of his letter. "Since our orders prohibiting it, there has been no music in this chapel, any more than in the other, excepting only one Sunday's afternoon, that in my absence at Glasgow, and that without any the least concurrence of mine, they had in this chapel a *trial of their music*, at which a good many persons of both congregations were present." There was a school of music. The Bishop continues: "It was represented to me that this school might be useful to the children, and might be a preparation for the time when we should see proper to introduce music into our chapels, which we ourselves were inclined to do as soon as we should see it prudent. The only proper answer that I thought I could give to this was, that they might have as many schools of music as they pleased, but that there would be no music in the chapel, until we should have our superior's full approbation. And to this, you may be persuaded, I have most strictly adhered, which was, certainly, no more than my duty." Bishop Hay in his reply acknowledged that he had been falsely informed, and that the coadjutor's "explication of the matter was perfectly satisfying."

CAP. XLII.

FRIENDSHIP OF MGR. ERSKINE—BISHOP GEDDES' JOURNEY TO THE ORKNEYS—HE DINES WITH THE MAGISTRATES OF KIRKWALL—VISITS CULLODEN MOOR—600 MILES OF WALKING—THE EFFORT TOO GREAT—THE "BEGINNING OF THE END"—THE NEW CHURCH AT PRESHOME OPENED ON PENTECOST SUNDAY, MAY 23RD, 1789—CONCERN ABOUT THE SCOTCH COLLEGE AT PARIS—DISORDER AT DOUAI—SCRUPLES OF MR. MENZIES—BOOKS REQUIRED BY BISHOP HAY—DESIRE FOR LARGER CHURCHES—REQUEST OF BISHOP M'DONALD FOR A COADJUTOR—500 CATHOLICS GONE TO PRINCE EDWARD'S ISLAND—600 MORE TO FOLLOW—A PRIEST APPOINTED FOR P. E. ISLAND—BISHOP HAY KINDLY RECEIVED BY THE DUKE OF GORDON AND THE EARL OF FINDLATER—A FRIENDLY EPISCOPALIAN MINISTER—A PROPOSAL OF MGR. CAMERON, RECTOR AT VALLADOLID, REJECTED.

It afforded much consolation to Bishop Geddes at this time to receive a complimentary letter from Monsignor Erskine, by which the worthy prelate showed his friendly recollection of his former school-fellows who were now in Scotland. He desired to be recalled to the kind and affectionate remembrance of Bishop Geddes, and prayed him when he should see Bishop Hay or any of his ancient comrades, to express to them his best wishes and compliments.

Bishop Geddes' many occupations could not divert him from his purpose of visiting for their comfort, his converts in the Orkneys. Bishop Hay was rather averse to his undertaking so long a journey, and doubted even whether Orkney were in the Lowland district. He did not, however, offer any hindrance and gave him the benefit of his prayers, wishing him a safe journey and a speedy return. He left Glasgow June 11th, in the evening, and passing through the romantic scenery of Stirlingshire and Perthshire, reached Fort Augustus on Lochness, in about ten days. While reading his office among the wild mountain passes of the Grampian range, his pious soul seemed to perceive new meaning in the words of the three children, *Benedicite montes et colles domino*. At the same time he was greatly distressed to observe the desolation of wide tracts of country, lately depopulated to make way for sheep farms. In Inverness-shire he found an old friend, a sister of Rev. John Reid, who was married to a sheep farmer, with whom he spent a pleasant Sunday. From Fort Augustus he passed through Glenmorriston and Strathglass ; thence, by Fasnakyle, to

Beauly, where he entered Ross-shire. By Dingwall
and Tain he skirted along the coast to John O'Groat's
house, the most northern point of the Scotch mainland, which he reached on the last day of June,
without fatigue and in excellent health. He crossed
the Pentland frith on July 1st, when a walk of ten
or twelve miles interrupted by two smaller ferries,
brought him to the mainland of Orkney, whence he
crossed over to Kirkwall early in the morning of the
following day. The weather was extremely fine,
and before sailing for the Island of Sanda, where his
friends resided, he wrote to Bishop Hay a narrative
of his journey up to that date. "Just now," he says
in his letter, "from the table where I write, I have
the Cathedral, quite entire, over against me. What
reflections! He hoped to reach Sanda the same
evening, and then, on the festival of the Visitation, to
begin his visit to his friends, on the most northerly spot
he ever expected to reach." On his arrival at Sanda,
the most northern but one of the Orkney Islands,
the good Bishop found his friends in deep distress.
Mr. Trail, the husband of one of them, was
dangerously ill of fever. In eight days he became
speechless, but was still in possession of all his senses.
He took the Bishop's hand and kissed it, expressing
a desire that he would pray with him. These signs,
together with the sick man's well known esteem for

the Catholic religion, encouraged the Bishop to give him absolution, and he soon after expired. The very delicate circumstances of the Bishop's visit had prevented him from speaking sooner to his host. Besides, Mr. Trail's brother, a minister, was daily expected to arrive from Westra. He was not without hope, nevertheless, that his presence had been of some service to the soul of his host, although at the last moment. He was able at least to give some consolation to the bereaved lady, who with her little girl, three years of age, and her sister, Miss Chapman, in the course of a few weeks, bade adieu to Orkney and took up her residence at Edinburgh.

It says much for the improving spirit of the time that the Bishop, on his return, dined with the magistrates of Kirkwall and was entertained by them with the greatest civility. He had the pleasure also to meet there some of his Edinburgh friends, who had arrived for the election. It is well known that the accomplished prelate was interested in everything connected with the history of his native land. It is no matter of surprise, therefore, that he spent some two or three hours on the fateful moor of Culloden. In the first week of August he was with Bishop Hay at Scalan. In less than eight weeks he had walked, as nearly as may be calculated, six hundred miles. The effort was too great. 'He was unwilling to admit it ; but his friends observed that he had sustained serious and lasting injury from over exertion. It was "the beginning of the end" of an unusually bright career. Once more only active service on behalf of the mission was in store for him ; then years of growing infirmity and severe suffering, which he bore with all the patience of a martyr, and then his well-won rest.

The new church at Preshome was now complete, and solemnly opened on Pentecost Sunday, May 23rd.

The good Baronet of Letterfourie, who had done so much towards forwarding the building did not live to enjoy the fruit of his zealous labours. He was found dead in bed on the morning of 30th of April. Mr. Mathieson had seen him two days before his death, when he never seemed in better health, or more full of plans and projects. They remained in conversation till midnight. The funeral was attended by the Duke of Gordon, the Earl of Findlater and sixteen other gentlemen. Although Bishop Hay at one time pronounced the plan of the new church a romantic scheme, he now acknowledged, after having examined the completed building, that it was indeed a beautiful house and well executed. He sincerely prayed God to grant long and peaceable possession. No church of the like pretentions had been erected in Scotland since the "Reformation." In the elegance and spaciousness of its internal proportions, it remains unsurpassed even till now by any other building of the kind in the country. A tablet over the principal entrance, towards the west, intimates its dedication, Dec. 1788, the year in which the foundation-stone was laid.

The revolution of France, which was now in progress, caused great anxiety to the Bishops on account of the college property held there. Mr. Farquarson represented so strongly the imminent danger of losing the Scotch establishment at Douai, that Bishop Hay, at his request, addressed the Bishop of the diocese, recommending the college to his protection. As regarded the college at Paris, Principal Gordon took steps such as were to be expected of him, by which he showed his determination to acknowledge no dependence on the Scotch Bishops. He communicated directly with the British Government. In consequence of his application, a despatch was addressed by the Duke of Leeds to Lord Robert Fitzgerald, the British *charge d'affaires* in Paris, instructing him to present a memorial to the French Government, if circumstances should render it necessary, on behalf of the Scotch College, Paris. He should represent the college as having long been property vested in British subjects ; and if it were no longer practicable to retain possession of it the British

Minister should endeavour to prevail on the French Government to allow the members of the college to dispose of their property and withdraw from the country, taking its value along with them. The Minister was authorized, moreover, to assure the French Government that their acquiescence would be exceedingly agreeable to his British Majesty and the nation. Such precautions were by no means uncalled for. The Scotch colleges, the Nuncio at Paris informed Cardinal Antonelli, were really in imminent danger. The Carthusians were no more; Grisi (the Scotch College), had no Superior but Principal Gordon. Mr, Thomson blames him for including his own college only in his application to the French Government. But as he was responsible only for it, more could not have been fairly expected. The guardians of other Scotch property in France might take measures on their own account.

Mr. Farquarson's account of the disorder which prevailed for some time at Douai, is of great value as illustrative of the sad results of the French revolution. "The most tyrannical Government," he observes, "is preferable to none at all. Better live under a Nero than be daily exposed to all the wild horrors of anarchy.

"Since the middle of May (he writes on July 5,) we are fairly at the mercy of our military. They hold courts martial, dismiss whom they please, insult openly their officers and the clergy. For three days and four nights on end, the town exhibited an image of hell. Four thousand armed drunken soldiers, with impunity rioted all over, entered communities, forced nunneries, made their quarters good everywhere, and yet, to their honour be it said, no indecencies were committed. Our good nuns were greatly frightened at such nocturnal visits. Some seminarists were roughly handled, and one, in particular, for making a difficulty in joining the rioters, received a thrust which would have been mortal, had not the point of the sword met with a rib. The English students were repeatedly dragged through the streets, whilst my youths happily escaped. Similar disgraceful scenes have been repeated, though in a less degree. The students have in a great measure abandoned the town during the last ten days. Owing to the great exertions of our municipal officers we have enjoyed peace ; but we are much afraid of the approaching 14th of July. At present about 1,200 electors for the *assemblée du departement*, fixed at Douai, are in town. Upon their choice our happiness greatly depends." Mr. Farquarson corresponded with the Bishop of Rhodez, a member of the National Assembly, on the subject of the Scotch College. That prelate showed himself a true friend at this critical period. With his concurrence Mr. Farquarson forwarded to Scotland a memorial to the Assembly, on behalf of the Scotch College at Douai, for the signatures of the Bishops and influential Catholic laymen, the Bishop of Rhodez undertaking to present it and to exert all his influence in its support. Principal Gordon's memorial to the French Government had been presented to the Assembly, and thence referred to the *comite ecclesiastique*.

Bishop Geddes undertook to obtain signatures; and he met with no hindrance till he came to Mr. Menzies of Pitfodels, who objected to the words *glorieuse memoire*, as applied to Louis XIV. He also criticised an expression which seemed to imply that the Catholic body in Scotland was still persecuted on account of religion. This difficulty was easily overcome by underlining the word *alors*, which immediately preceded the phrase in question. The other difficulty, even, was ultimately got over; and the good man whose scrupulous honour remained sensitive as that of a child, added his signature. Eleven signatures, in addition to those of the Bishops, were obtained, and the memorial was immediately despatched to Douai.

The meeting at Scalan could not be held so early as usual this year, Bishop McDonald being detained at home by illness. Bishop Hay, meanwhile, requested his coadjutor to procure for him at Edinburgh, the following books : Reid on Human Nature, some copies of English controversial works, Sir John Dalrymple's Memoirs, and a correct edition of Cicero's Epistles and Philosophical Works. The Bishop's studies, it would appear, were not confined to books, for he ordered, at the same time, two or three glass prisms, a conical bottle with a flat bottom, and a cure for the *morbus pedicularis*, used by a Mrs. Smith, with whom the boys lately returned to Scalan, lodged at Edinburgh.

There was a desire among the clergy for larger and more commodious churches ; this was opposed by the Bishop on the ground of expense which could be very ill afforded. "We are not content nowadays," he said, " with moderate beginnings, and bettering things by degrees ; but we must have all our conveniences at once." For the present necessities of Mr. Pepper's chapel at Dundee, notwithstanding, he contributed £5.

Bishop Macdonald arrived at Scalan in the beginning of September. Business was then at once proceeded with. In the letters to Rome, mention was made of Bishop Geddes' journey of some 600 miles on foot to visit his converts in Orkney, Bishop Macdonald also represented to Cardinal Antonelli his failing health and his great fatigue in travelling over his scattered district, and among distant islands, requesting permission to have a coadjutor. His request was sustained, also, in consequence of the difficulties that lately occurred in England, owing to the death of two of the Bishops before successors had been provided. He informed the Scotch agent at Rome, in a private letter, that 500 Catholics had lately emigrated to St. John's Island (now Prince Edward's) and Quebec; and that 600 of South Uist were ready to follow them in the spring. This emigration greatly diminished their congregations, and some of the Highland missionary priests were in consequence, reduced to great distress. A sufficient number of their flocks remained to require their ministry; but these were themselves among the very poorest. Thus, Mr. Norman MacDonald, "a deserving clergyman," with his pittance of £12 a year, had to support his mother, his sister and his niece, since the departure of the most substantial amongst his people, the preceding summer. The emigrants to America, meanwhile, were not left spiritually destitute. The Bishop, yielding to the importunities of the Highland settlers in St. John's Island, had permitted Mr. Angus McEachern, "a valuable young man," to go out to them. They also succeeded in obtaining the ministry of a promising young priest from Halifax.

When the meeting was over Bishop Hay paid a visit to the Duke of Gordon, who was staying at his shooting lodge of Glenfiddich. Both the Duke and his guest, the Earl of Findlater, showed the kindest attentions to the Bishop. His Grace promised to visit Scalan, but when the time came was prevented by the severe weather.

Bishop Geddes concurred with the Bishop in regard to his protest against excessive expense in new churches. Nevertheless, he thought it not unreasonable that Catholics should have their places of worship in a condition suited to the progress of the time. The chapel at Edinburgh was now too small ; and the people expressed their desire to have a larger one. But the Bishop might rely on it that his coadjutor would enter on no such undertaking until sufficient means were at his disposal. It is characteristic of the better times that a Protestant minister, Dr. Webster, who was erecting a fine Episcopalian chapel beyond the infirmary, urged Bishop Geddes to take the second storey above his chapel for a Catholic place of worship. In the event of his consenting, Dr. Webster offered to erect a cupola. Bishop Geddes thanked him ; but declined the offer. The doctor was not satisfied with this refusal, and insisted that the matter should be referred to Bishop Hay. As was to be expected, Bishop Hay, whilst he thanked the liberal minister for his kind offer, and sent to him his compliments, expressed his regret that circumstances were such at the time as to prevent him from accepting it.

Mr. Cameron, in writing from Valladolid, informed Bishop Geddes that it would not be possible to receive any more students till 1792, in consequence of the expenses incurred in building a small country house in the vineyard, together with the loss occasioned by the late bad years. This resolution the Bishop strongly condemned. When the need of priests was so great the want of them was surely of more consequence than some delay in paying a small debt. The Bishop ought not to yield to Mr. Cameron in this matter. If Bishop McDonald concurred, he would certainly send boys when others came home; and if Mr. Cameron should send them back, he must abide the consequences. "It was really a shame," he said, writing to Bishop Geddes, "that there should be such a proposal, and I intend you to write to Mr. Cameron strongly on the subject."

CAP. XLIII.

PORTUGUESE STUDENTS—BISHOP HAY AND SCALAN—
GLASGOW—VALLADOLID—COUNTRY SCHOOLS—
SCOTCH COLLEGES IN FRANCE—THE STEWART
PAPERS—THE BISHOP OF RHODEZ THANKED—
FAVOUR OF THE FRENCH ASSEMBLY TO THE SCOTCH
COLLEGES — RE-PUBLICATION OF BISHOP HAY'S
WORKS—BISHOP GEDDES' EXCESS OF DUTY—CON-
SECRATION OF THE FIRST AMERICAN BISHOP AT
LULWORTH CASTLE—MR. BURKE'S "REFLECTIONS
ON THE FRENCH REVOLUTION"—BISHOP HAY
CONCERNED ABOUT THE SCOTCH COLLEGE AT PARIS
—THE "SINCERE CHRISTIAN" MUCH DESIRED IN
SCOTLAND — BISHOP GEDDES AND GLASGOW —
DECREASE OF PREJUDICE—TENNIS COURT AS A
CHAPEL — DIFFICULTY OF FINDING PRIESTS —
BISHOP HAY STILL AT SCALAN—WHAT WAS TAUGHT
IN CHARITY SCHOOLS—DREAD OF REVOLUTIONARY
CONTAGION SPREADING TO GREAT BRITAIN —
BISHOP HAY AND DR. REID'S PHILOSOPHY—SIR
JOHN DALRYMPLE'S HISTORICAL WORK—BISHOP
HAY AND MR. BAGNALL—COMPETENT TEACHERS
FOUND FOR CATHOLIC SCHOOLS.

Something truly new in the history of the mission comes now to be recorded. Five young students arrived from Portugal in order to prosecute their medical studies at Edinburgh. They were shortly afterwards followed by two more who had previously been to Denmark for a similar purpose. The Intendant General of Police at Lisbon had availed himself of the mediation of Mr. William Fryer, Superior of the English College there, for securing Bishop Geddes' co-operation in the arrangements intended to be made for the accommodation of the students. Mr. Fryer, accordingly corresponded with Bishop Geddes on the subject. The young men were to be sent at the expense of a charitable institution in which the Queen of Portugal took a deep interest. A house was to be taken for them, servants engaged and Bishop Geddes appointed Superior of their establishment. Board and lodgings were to be provided for him and a pension of 1,000 crowns a year, on his undertaking to superintend the temporal and spiritual affairs of the young men. Decency, rather than elegance, was to be studied in their table and their dress; and they were to be kept close to their work. Any idle or refractory members of the party were to be sent home at once. Notwithstanding the unexpected increase of his cares and responsibilities, the Bishop felt that he could not wholly decline the proposal, although it was impossible that he should reside in the same house with the young men. It was, therefore, arranged that he should render whatever service was in his power in forwarding the scheme. His reputation had long ago extended from Madrid to Lisbon, so that her Portuguese Majesty, on hearing that he had consented to undertake a general superintendence of the plan, expressed the highest satisfaction, and it was settled that the Bishop's allowance should be equivalent to £110 a year in English money. He took a house for the young men in Chessel's court, Canongate, and early in October they began to reside there. In communicating the details of the affair to his friend at Scalan, he was not without fear that this new addition to his anxieties would not be approved. It was inevitable, however; and hoping that Providence would so direct it as to be serviceable to the common good, he commended it and himself to his friend's good prayers.

The Bishop, in his reply on the subject of the Portuguese colony, expressed his sense of the honour done to Scotland, and of the probable advantage to the mission; but regretted that his friend should be burdened with a charge so foreign to his principal duties. "It will require a great deal of time," he said, "and attention to keep these young students in proper order and preserve their morals in that corrupted place and dangerous study. May God Almighty assist. The Queen, indeed, has been very generous to you. I pray God to enable you to employ it properly. I make no doubt but the design of Heaven in sending you that supply is to enable you to co-operate with me in placing the missions on an independent footing, and providing for all its difficulties ; and I hope you will always have that end in view." The Bishop further advised that the increase of income should remain a profound secret; "for if friends came to know of it, he would be pestered without mercy, *experto crede*."

Bishop Hay now entertained the hope that he would be able to render Scalan available not only for the supply of foreign colleges, but also as a seminary for training even to the highest step ; and he made arrangements for securing the maintenance of twelve students permanently. He requested that Mr. Thomson would contribute towards this purpose. He asked him in the meantime only to send to him a supply of school books. Such of the classics as required purgation were not to be had in Scotland in a purified form. Could Mr. Thomson, therefore, find some copies of Terence and Ovid's Metamorphoses expurgated. Such would be most acceptable. Rollin had praised a work entitled *Terentius Christianus*. If Mr. Thomson could find a copy, he might be good enough to send it, together with any of Cicero's Philosophical Works with good notes. For the

Bishop's own use he would be glad to have Boservich's Conic sections.

Bishop Geddes, on visiting Glasgow, found that everything there was proceeding to his satisfaction. The house in which the Catholics met had been leased for another year ; and Mr. Wilson, the landlord, had permitted the partitions to be removed. It was gratifying also to Bishop Hay to learn from his friend that Mr. Menzies had returned from the excursion for the benefit of his health, tolerably restored, and that the seven Portuguese students had arrived on 21st October. He, at the same time, assured the Bishop that whatever money he could command, should, with very few necessary expenses, be applied to the great end which both of them had chiefly at heart. He recommended that Bishop Hay should treat in a friendly manner with Mr Cameron at Valladolid about taking boys the following year. The new bishops for England, he added, were Mr. Douglas, *cæsareæ in partibus* for London, and Mr. Wm. Gibson, *accaviten* for the North. Again November 11th, Bishop Geddes wrote to his friend. Referring to the state of the country schools, he said that he had lately the satisfaction of setting matters to rights. One evening at supper, meeting a Mr. Kemp, a clerical gentleman officially connected with the management of schools, he proposed to him that the

Catholic children should not be required to learn the assembly catechism in the charity schools. The company at once joined the Bishop in saying that it was a hardship. Mr. Kemp evaded this direct appeal, humourously remarking that he was not endowed with dispensing power. Two other ministers and a lady supported the Bishop's plea. At parting Mr. Kemp took him by the hand and said that in company he felt under some restraint, but that he wished to have some private conversation with the Bishop, and to settle the matter in an amicable manner. It was understood that Mr. Fleming would be removed to some distance from the braes of Glenlivat.

It was not long till Bishop Geddes had more news to communicate (Nov. 15th). A decree of the French Assembly, dated 28th October, was in favour of the Scotch Colleges in France. Mr. Andrew Stewart had mentioned the Scotch College in Paris to Mr. Pitt and the Duke of Leeds, and had prevailed on them to send a despatch to the British Minister at Paris on the subject. The National Assembly of France founded their decree for leaving the Scotch colleges there as they were, on the ground that they did not belong to the French nation. It was news to Bishop Hay that a project was on foot for the purchase of the papers belonging to the Paris College by the British nation ; and Mr. Pitt, it was said, was inclined to treat generously. Bishop Hay, writing to Bishop Geddes, suggested that he should let Mr. Andrew Stewart know that the Stewart papers at Grisi (the Scotch College) were not the property of that college, but only a deposit, and that their owners were the Scotch Catholics as a body. The Bishop had heard that the papers left by the Archbishop of Glasgow were to be returned to Glasgow if religion should ever be restored in Scotland. Part of the price to be paid for those papers might perhaps be allotted to the mission. But the Bishop was quite aware of the extreme delicacy of the negotiation; and he only suggested it as deserving his friend's consideration.

The Bishops of Scotland offered to the Bishop of Rhodez, their common thanks for the active interest which he had taken in the national colleges. The reply of that Prelate was forwarded from Douai by Mr. Farquarson. It expressed his friendly feelings, and held out good hopes of success.

The memorial regarding the national colleges in France, to which Bishop Geddes obtained signatures among the Catholic gentry, prevailed with the French Assembly; and the provision to Douai was voted permanent. Archbishop Troy of Dublin, writing to Bishop Geddes, begged of him to present his respects to Bishop Hay, and to assure him of his " unutterable esteem;" adding "I have encouraged the re-publication of his Polemical Tracts here. They have rendered signal service to the cause of religion. The second Dublin edition of the *Sincere, Devout,* and *Pious Christian* is now in my printer's press, and will be speedily published. The *Scripture Doctrine on Miracles* was published last year."

The rapid failure of Rev. Mr. Menzies' health, together with Rev. Mr. Robertson's illness of several weeks' duration, laid on Bishop Geddes an excess of parochial duty; and to this was added his care of the Portuguese students. He found time, notwithstanding, for correspondence with his friends. Writing to Mr. Thomson, Dec. 18th, he informed him of the consecration of Bishop Caryl (Carroll), for America, at Lulworth Castle, on the Feast of the Assumption; and also, that Mr. Burke's *Reflections on the French Revolution* had been well received, 15,000 copies having been sold in a few weeks. Bishop Geddes considered that, notwithstanding the opposition which it met with, this able work was likely to do much good in view of the state of matters which then prevailed.

In the event of the Scotch College at Paris being preserved, a new constitution would be necessary. This was decidedly the opinion of Bishop Hay; and it caused him no slight anxiety. The Prior of the

Carthusians was deprived of his office, and were the masters who had been under his authority, to be subject to no control ? The Bishop maintained that unless the College were placed under the authority of the Scotch Bishops it would never be of much service to the mission.

Writing to Bishop Geddes, he requested him on the first opportunity to return his most respectful compliments to the Archbishop of Dublin, adding " It is a comfort to think that my small endeavours are doing good anywhere." Copies of the *Sincere Christian* were much wanted in Scotland, and the Bishop thought that 200 might be procured from Dublin at a cheaper rate than they could be printed at in Scotland.

The important mission of Glasgow will now for a few moments engage our attention. The second and third Sundays after Epiphany, Bishop Geddes was there on a pastoral visit. There were twenty-nine communicants. Among the small congregation were observed, with pleasure, five or six soldiers in uniform. Some Protestants of note, and, among others, the Procurator fiscal, wished to be present at Mass. But Bishop Geddes thought it more prudent to ask them not to come, as their presence might excite too much attention. It appeared to him, besides, that they were moved with curiosity. It is more remarkable

that some of the wealthier merchants declared in
private company their willingness to contribute towards the maintenance of a Catholic priest in the
town. This they proposed in order to show the
world that they were not so bigotted in Glasgow as
was generally supposed. Mr. Wilson, town clerk and
proprietor of the house in which the Catholics assembled, assured the Bishop, one night, in the course of
a long conversation, that prejudices against Catholics
had subsided within the previous three or four years,
more completely than he could have thought, at one
time, possible. As regarded the mercantile and
manufacturing classes, this was so far a mistake, as
their decrease of bigotry must in great measure be
ascribed to a cause very different from any advance
which they had made in true liberality. Motives of
self-interest were at work. The late Dr. Cleland,
who was by no means Catholic although he lived on
terms of friendship with his kinsman, Bishop Hay,
formally testifies that, when in 1791, the great tide
of emigration from the North Highlands threatened
to drain the country of its hardy mountaineers, Messrs.
Geo. McIntosh, David Dale, Robert Dalgleish and
some others of the capitalist manufacturers, invited
the Highlanders to Glasgow ; and, as an inducement
to the Catholics amongst them, promised security in
the practice of their religious worship. This they

could not have done at a very much earlier period ; and when they did so encourage the Catholic Highlanders, the tide of bigotry among the citizens, generally, must have ceased to flow with its ancient vigour. On occasion of the pastoral visit just referred to, the Tennis Court of Mitchell Street, was first taken on lease, as a temporary chapel. Bishop Hay received with the greatest pleasure, these accounts from Glasgow; and they gave him cause to hope that God in His mercy would give religion a footing in that city. But he found it very difficult to supply spiritual aid there and in other places.

Bishop Geddes had some difficulty in providing funds for the travelling expenses of students on their way to the foreign colleges. Bishop Hay made him welcome to any money of his, that happened to be available, until a supply should come. He hoped, at the same time, that the dividend of the Bank of Scotland would be considerable. The difficulty of supplying priests for vacant missions gave the Bishop much concern. Bishop Hay was now himself unable to undertake the laborious duties of a mission ; and he thought it best to remain at Scalan which, otherwise, would require the services of an able priest in the vigour of his years. Besides, none could carry out so well as himself the reforms which he had inaugurated at the Seminary; and he hoped to render it a lasting benefit to the mission.

Bishop Geddes had lately had some friendly conversations with Mr. Kemp, who had promised to exempt Catholic children from learning the catechism of the Presbyterian Assembly, acknowledging that it was not suited for the instruction of young or ignorant persons. Catholic children in the charity schools should be taught only reading, writing and arithmetic, whilst, with regard to religion, it was sufficient that they should be made acquainted with the morality and history of the Scriptures, especially of the Gospels. Mr. Kemp had a plan in view for this purpose, which the Bishop thought not a bad one. It was to draw up a set of proper questions without subjoining the answers, but only indicating the chapters where they could be found, so that the children might look for themselves. In order the better to enable him to carry out his plan, the Bishop gave him Challoner's History of the Old and New Testaments, and Fleury's Catechism. Mr. Kemp promised to avoid everything that was in controversy between Catholics and Protestants. On these conditions being agreed to, the Bishop engaged to do all in his power to cause the charity schools to be frequented by Catholic children. He was confident that Bishop Hay would approve of all that he had done.

Bishop Hay's perusal of Mr. Burke's work on the French Revolution filled his mind with too well-founded alarm. The statesman's dread of the revolutionary contagion spreading to Great Britain caused him to push his conclusions to their utmost limits. It so appeared to the Bishop, to whom many of the facts alleged were altogether new. But, assuming their truth, which it was impossible to doubt, attested as it was by so great an authority as Mr. Burke, the Bishop acknowledged that he was deeply affected by the state of the French nation, and considered its misery as one of the heaviest judgments that, to his knowledge, had ever been inflicted on a people. The condition of France, in general, naturally excited in his mind the keenest anxiety for the safety of the Scotch Colleges there. He dreaded, especially, the kind of instruction which would probably be provided to the universities; and if the civic oath should be imposed on the superiors of colleges, what might not be feared? Might not their refusal to take it be made a pretext for annuling the seminaries and seizing their properties? He communicated to his coadjutor the vain wish that the Scotch property in France were withdrawn from that doomed country.

The study of Dr. Reid's philosophy was more pleasing. The Bishop was attracted to a second perusal of this author's work on the intellectual powers. He regretted, however, that there should be anything in a work of such distinguished merit that was calculated to lessen the author's claim on the esteem of every intelligent reader. He could wish, therefore, that in a future edition, Dr. Reid would correct the assertion that Malebranche was a Jesuit, which he puts forward with a view to account for Arnauld's opposition to the French philosophers. Malebranche was an Oratorian, and his associates were, in general, united in sentiments with Arnauld's party in their controversy with the Jesuits. A passage on Transubstantiation, in Dr. Reid's work, was another source of vexation to the Bishop. Every well-informed Catholic could not but preceive that the professor wrote without knowledge of the subject. It would not be difficult to show, according to his own principles, that nothing is more consistent with his theory of philosophy than the Catholic doctrine regarding the great mystery. The Bishop desired, also, to have sent to him Dr. Reid's Treatise on the Active Powers. He greatly valued Sir John Dalrymple's historical work, which the author had lately presented to him; and charged the coadjutor to express his warmest thanks for the valuable gift, not failing to say that it gave him real pleasure to find that he still had a place in Sir John's remembrance.

The friendly consideration and sound judgment of Bishop Hay were well shown by an arrangement which he made with Mr. Bagnal, a manufacturer at Glasgow, of Staffordshire pottery. The Bishop held bonds of this manufacturer on account of several sums of money which he had advanced to him. It was agreed that Mr. Bagnal should provide a complete assortment of stone ware for the seminary, and a double set of such things as were most in use ; and that on this being done all his bonds should be returned to him discharged. This was the most easy way in which the bonds could be cancelled ; and the Bishop was anxious to have the matter settled in case of difficulty arising after his death.

It was not sufficient to take measures for preventing Catholic children from being imbued with Presbyterian ideas at schools that were held under the auspices of the Kirk. The time was now come when there could be schools exclusively devoted to the education of Catholic children. The chief difficulty appeared to be that of finding properly qualified masters. The teacher whom Bishop Hay had appointed at Glenlivat failed. An Irish scholar whom Bishop Geddes employed at Edinburgh was alike unfortunate. Both Bishops at last succeeded in finding competent teachers for Edinburgh, Glenlivat and Aberdeen.

CAP. XLIV.

CHURCH OF FRANCE REVOLUTIONIZED—BISHOP HAY ENCOURAGES THE SCHOOLS UNDER CHARGE OF MR. KEMP—MORE THAN USUAL PROGRESS AT GLASGOW—34 CONVERTS—BISHOP GEDDES' EFFORTS TO CONCILIATE PRINCIPAL GORDON—RAPID SALE OF BISHOP HAY'S WORKS AT DUBLIN—REJOICING OF ENGLISH CATHOLICS ON PASSING OF THE RELIEF BILL—OATH UNEXCEPTIONABLE—THE "CATHOLIC COMMITTEE" NULLIFIED—BISHOP HAY AND DR. REID—INFLUENTIAL CONVERSIONS—RELIEF BILL GIVES JOY AT ROME—THE POPE'S SATISFACTION—MEETINGS OF 1791 AT GIBSTON—CESSATION OF PERSECUTION—CHURCHES MULTIPLYING ALL OVER THE COUNTRY—2,000 CATHOLIC HIGHLANDERS EMIGRATE TO CANADA AND PRINCE EDWARD'S ISLAND—NECESSITY OF SUPPORT FROM CONGREGATIONS—THE SAME BEGUN—MR. JOHN CHISHOLM, COADJUTOR TO BISHOP M'DONALD—THE SCOTCH COLLEGES IN FRANCE—BISHOP GEDDES GOES TO PARIS WITH FULL POWERS—ASSISTED BY THE BRITISH AMBASSADOR AND THE PAPAL CHARGE D'AFFAIRES—MET FRIENDS IN LONDON — MR. GEORGE CHALMERS PRESENTS HIM WITH A PORTRAIT OF QUEEN MARY

CATHOLICS OF SCOTLAND. 539

—LORD LOUGHBOROUGH—THE KING JAMES' PAPERS
—ECCENTRICITY OF PRINCIPAL GORDON—CASE OF
COLLEGE SUBMITTED TO ARBITERS—DECISION IN
FAVOUR OF THE BISHOPS—THE PRINCIPAL STILL
HOLDS OUT—BISHOP GEDDES OBTAINS POSSESSION
OF THE ORIGINAL DEED OF FOUNDATION—PRIOR
OF THE CARTHUSIANS, CHIEF SUPERIOR OF THE
COLLEGE, FAVOURS BISHOP GEDDES---BISHOP GEDDES
DISTRESSED BY THE SAD STATE OF FRANCE—PRIN-
CIPAL GORDON YIELDS AT LAST, ABANDONS THE
COLLEGE AND GOES TO LONDON.

Bishop Geddes entertained pretty much the same opinion as Bishop Hay in regard to Mr. Burke and the French Revolution. That eminent statesman, he thought, however, was a little too declamatory; but the substance of his work was very just. In France, the Church even was revolutionized. The Bishops of Autun, Orleans and Sens alone remained steadfast. For the time there was a deplorable schism; but it was not destined to be of long continuance.

Bishop Hay was so highly pleased with Mr. Kemp's liberal conduct in regard to Catholics attending charity schools under his charge, that he proposed to him that he should establish a school for the poorer population of Glenlivat. Provided that the same promise in regard to the Catholics as was made at Edinburgh, were adhered to, the Bishop would undertake or encourage the people to send their children to the school, and would himself subscribe something in aid of its funds. He, moreover, invited Mr. Kemp to make Scalan his home when he should visit that part of the country.

Bishop Geddes' pastoral visit of ten days to Glasgow this summer was attended with more than its usual fruit. Conversions were, as yet, but few and far between, even in the missions that were longest established, or were, in their humble way, a continuation of the ancient state of things. There were no fewer than thirty-four converts received on occasion of the visit referred to. Where the congregation was always increasing, there could not fail to be a few baptisms. Only five were ready for baptism since the former visit.

Bishop Hay, acting on the suggestion of his coadjutor, communicated with the Nuncio and the Prior of the Carthusians at Paris, requesting their assistance and protection in behalf of Douai College. In the event of their answer being favourable, he intended to make a like request for the college at Paris. He also despatched a procuration in his own name, and that of his coadjutor, for Principal Gordon, with whom he associated Messrs. Innes and Farquarson, the latter President of Douai College, and the former Prefect of Studies at Paris. Bishop Geddes, however, not unreasonably feared that the Principal might reject the proposal to give him associates, unless he were first consulted. He, accordingly, with a view to prepare the way for compliance, prayed him to forget the past and act solely for the good of religion in his own country.

It was highly satisfactory to the Bishops to learn, at this time, that the new Irish edition of Bishop Hay's works was selling rapidly at Dublin. There were seven volumes. Two hundred copies of the *Sincere Christian* were on the way to Scotland.

On his return to Scalan in July, Bishop Hay had just heard from London of the general rejoicing among the English Catholics at the passing of their Relief Bill. The oath appeared to him unexceptionable. Even Bishop Douglas made no objection to it. Not without a partial leaning to the side of the English Bishops, their Brother of Scotland could not avoid thinking that Providence had now fairly decided in favour of the Bishops against the "Catholic Committee" and its plans.

Painful feelings were once more aroused in the Bishop's mind as he read Dr. Reid's Treatise on the Active Powers, to find that a man of Reid's abilities and penetration should lose himself so often and so completely in speaking against the Catholic tenets in a manner which showed that he was writing on what he knew nothing about.

The coadjutor had now to inform Bishop Hay that Principal Gordon refused to act with the associates whom the Bishop had proposed to him. It was consoling, meanwhile, to learn that there were some conversions among the more influential classes. Two ladies of good family, Mrs. Glendonwyn of Parton and Mrs. Goldie were reconciled to the Church.

Mr. Thomson, before the end of the month of July, informed Bishop Hay that the English Relief Bill caused universal rejoicing at Rome. It was held to be of such importance that the Pope expressed his satisfaction to the Cardinals assembled on St. Peter's Day.

Early in the following month of this year (August 1791), the three Scotch Bishops, together with the administrators, held the annual meeting at Gibston, near Huntley. In their letters to Rome they imparted to Propaganda the pleasing information that the pressure of persecution had ceased in Scotland; and that chapels or churches were multiplying all over the country; but that, on the other hand, emigration was thinning the ranks of the Catholics. Two thousand Catholic Highlanders had departed for Canada and St. John's Island. Such emigration, no doubt, favoured the progress of the Catholic religion in America; but it was no groundless fear, on the part of the Bishops, that it might prove detrimental to the state of religion at home. The difficulty of maintaining the clergy had long been felt; and now, accordingly, the Bishop began to induce the people to contribute towards their support. This was a great step; and it was not without good results. A measure so new to the congregations would require time and much prudence.

Bishop McDonald's request to have a coadjutor having been favourably received, he now suggested that Mr. John Chisholm, a worthy priest in the district of Strathglass, should be appointed to the office. This was Bishop McDonald's last meeting with his brethren. Deafness, always increasing, gave pain to his colleagues; but he himself bore the infirmity with exemplary patience. The meeting was a very agreeable one. The utmost harmony prevailed; and Bishop Hay, in consequence, showed himself remarkably cheerful.

In addition to the ordinary business of the annual meeting the Bishops found that it was incumbent on them to give their attention to the state of the national colleges in France. Matters were proceeding in that country in such a way as to give the greatest cause for alarm. It was resolved that Bishop Geddes should repair to France, as representing the interests of the Scotch mission at Douai and Paris. Bishop Geddes was at first opposed to this arrangement, although it had been urged, early in the year, by Messrs. Farquarson and Innes. He neither liked it, nor thought it practicable. Nevertheless, it was unanimously agreed upon at the meeting; and he consented to go and do his best. The affair of the Paris College was one of great delicacy, owing to the extraordinary part Principal Gordon had acted. Besides, it was not without personal danger for a British subject to appear at Paris in the midst of the agitations of the advancing revolution. The charge laid upon Bishop Geddes by the meeting was that he should receive, in the name of the Scotch Bishops and clergy, from the Prior of the Carthusians the property entrusted to his predecessors by Archbishop Beaton; that he should place the colleges at Paris and Douai on a satisfactory footing; and that, if necessary, he should sell their whole property and transfer its value elsewhere.

A formal commission was prepared for Bishop Geddes at Gibston. It gave him full power to treat with the National Assembly of France and all others whom it concerned regarding the colleges at Douai and Paris, their properties and all other property of the Scotch mission. The document bore the signatures of the two Vicars Apostolic, five administrators and four and twenty of the principal Catholic gentry of Scotland. The Bishop met with much civility when on his way to France. In London he enjoyed the hospitality of his friend, Bishop Douglas. He also met with special kindness on the part of the celebrated antiquary, George Chalmers, author of *Caledonia*. He speaks of Mr. Chalmers as a truly excellent man. He made him a present of a valuable print of Queen Mary. He learned that Lord Loughborough had been the principal agent in passing the Catholic Relief Bill : and another friend, Mr. Stewart, took him by invitation to dine with the Judge. He could not let pass so good an opportunity without expressing the gratitude of the Catholic body to His Lordship. The compliment was well received ; and he was invited to return to dinner next day, and to bring Bishop Douglas with him. They passed a very agreeable evening with Lord and Lady Loughborough alone. The Bishop did not fail to express a hope that something might, ere long, be done for the Scotch Catholics, now that their English friends had obtained so much relief. The King was, at the time, anxious to purchase the King James' papers, which were preserved in the Scotch College at Paris. Mr. Stewart took much interest in the negotiations and persuaded the Bishop to defer his departure for

France till they were completed. Mr. Chalmers undertook to bring them under the notice of Sir Jos. Banks and other trustees of the British Museum. Sir Joseph Banks promised, at Mr. Chalmers' request, to mention to the King, the subject of the Stewart papers, a matter in which the worthy and the learned were all concerned. Mr. Chalmers, in his letter of thanks to Bishop Hay, for forwarding the print of Queen Mary, paid a well deserved tribute to the merits of Bishop Geddes, in the most friendly words: "Alas! would I could have been more useful and kind to Bishop Geddes whose extraordinary merits entitle him to every possible attention. I would almost go to Paris myself, which, I think, has now few attractions, to ensure the success of his mission." On arriving at Douai, the Bishop found fifteen Scotch students in good health. They were pursuing their education under their own Prefect of Studies, and a professor of humanities, at home, owing to the disturbed state of the place; but there were fears lest they should be forced to attend the public schools; and this attempt must be resisted, as all the old professors had been expelled for refusing the constitutional oath.

The Bishop well knew how important it was to avoid an open rupture with Principal Gordon. He, therefore, addressed him in a mild and persuasive letter, earnestly praying him to agree to the plans of the Bishops and concert matters with them for the good of the college and religion in general. He wrote with firmness ; but was, at the same time, particularly friendly and warning. He recounted their past difference and explained the nature of the commission or procuration, which he had brought with him. He endeavoured, moreover, to show the Principal how groundless were his pretensions to independence, and how expedient and even necessary it was that the Bishops and the Principal should act together. Bishop Hay maintained that the Principal would not hold out long if he were managed with firmness ; or, if he did, he would probably commit himself to some extravagant plan which would

Bishops A second appeal were the better. God was highly offended at the commission entrusted to Bishop Geddes, and resented it in a very marked way by giving him to understand that he must not expect to be entertained in the Scotch College at Paris. The Bishop took up his residence in a private house, in which also lodged a member of the National Assembly, which was supposed to give additional security.

On approaching Paris, the Bishop found that there was much ferment and excitement, and that churchmen, especially, were in danger. His first proceeding was to communicate with the Prior of the Carthusians, and that in a friendly way, stating the nature of his errand and the dispute with the Principal as to the interference of the Scotch Bishops, and requesting the Prior to see that justice was done to the interests of religion in Scotland. The Prior was weak and undecided, although a good man; and he depended for his opinions on such matters, on an Irishman, a Canon of Charteris, who, fortunately, espoused the cause of the Scotch Bishops and carried the Prior along with him. In the next place the Bishop had an interview with the Principal. It was more friendly than his correspondence. He invited the Bishop twice to dinner, and by an express order of the Prior, offered him rooms in the College. But this offer, made in such circumstances, the Bishop thought proper to decline. Mr. Gordon, moreover, agreed to discuss the matter in a friendly way in presence of the Prior. If they could not come to an agreement, the Abbe de Floirac, Vicar-General of Paris, who, at the time, governed the diocese, and the Abbe de Rigaud, Visitor of the Carmelite Nuns, were, in that case, to be requested to arbitrate on the conflicting claims. Bishop Geddes prepared a summary of his proposals on behalf of the Scotch Bishops. It amounted to this: that the founder's will and the constitution of the College should be inspected; that the property of the College should not be sold, or its value removed elsewhere without the consent and approval of the Scotch Bishops; that, in the event of the Prior ceasing to be Superior of the Scotch College, the election of the Principal and of the Procurator of the College should, for the future, vest in the Scotch Bishops, together with the right to nominate students; and that a deputy of the Bishops should visit the College once a year, and inspect the Procurator's accounts.

Bishop Geddes was much assisted in his negotiations at Paris by the countenance of the British Ambassador, Lord Gower, to whom and to his wife, the Countess of Sutherland, he had letters of introduction.- They both showed him great civility. Through the recommendation, also, of Cardinal Zalada, the Roman Secretary of State, the Bishop found a willing and useful assistant in the Abbé Salomon, the Papal Chargé d'Affaires. He obtained still more effectual assistance from the cordial cooperation of Mgr. Colbert, Bishop of Rhodez, than from any other source. This Prelate was connected with Scotland by family ties, and had become familiar with the Scotch College at Paris during a residence of three years in it. Notwithstanding the obstacles and delays interposed by Mr. Gordon, the conference was held at last, before the arbiters. The deed of foundation and other original documents were produced and read; and the arbiters gave a unanimous decision against the claims of the Principal to independent jurisdiction in the College. Their decision not having the final authority of a judicial sentence, the Principal showed no inclination to yield. He addressed the Bishop of Rhodez in a long letter, in which he endeavoured to establish the independent position of the College and of himself. The Bishop took great pains to refute his conclusions in a voluminous reply. Mr. Gordon remained proof against reason, trusting to the unwillingness of his opponents to bring him into the courts of law, considering the disorganized state of French society at the time. The College, however, was safe as long as the Prior of the Carthusians remained, for he had undertaken to do nothing in regard to it without the consent of the Bishop of Rhodez and the approval of the Scotch Bishops. The College, besides, had influential friends on the spot, in the Bishop of Rhodez and the three Abbes who had acted as arbiters at the conference; they would not fail to keep the Scotch Bishops duly informed of everything that happened. Thus far the mission of Bishop Geddes had proved successful. But the Prior's tenure of life was very uncertain; and if he were removed, or if the Principal should regain his influence over him, all might be lost. If the Prior had acted with more vigour, more, probably, would have been gained. Bishop Geddes found an opportunity, and it was not without some value, of seeing and copying the original deed of foundation. From politeness, one evening, the Principal had allowed him to take it to his lodgings. But next morning, repenting of what he considered his rash courtesy, he called to get the deed back again. This mattered not; the Bishop had copied it over night. More than the Bishop had gained could not have been attempted in the unsettled state of affairs and on the eve of a threatened war with England. He, therefore, set about preparing to return home. He says little in his correspondence of the state of the Revolution. The deplorable condition to which the Church was reduced caused him great distress; but, at the same time, he was much consoled in witnessing "many examples of constancy in the faith, of patience, of piety and of every Christian virtue."

Principal Gordon, as the French Revolution was hastening to anarchy, guided by the instinct of self-preservation, determined to abandon the Scotch College, leaving it in charge of the college lawyer.

He gave notice to Mr. Innes, the Prefect of Studies to leave it in a fortnight. This, however, Mr. Innes refused to do. The Prior of the Carthusians, on appeal to him, disapproved of Mr. Gordon's act, and appointed Mr. Innes, Procurator. Mr. Gordon protested. But the Prior and Mr. Innes carried the case before the municipality, where they must have gained, if the Principal had not given way and placed the affairs of the College in the hands of Mr. Innes. The intractable Principal Gordon was then at liberty to seek safety in flight. He went to reside in London.

CAP. XLV.

BISHOP HAY, ALTHOUGH PROCURATOR, UNDERTAKES THE WHOLE PAROCHIAL DUTY OF EDINBURGH IN ADDITION TO HIS EPISCOPAL DUTIES — VISITS GLASGOW—MUCH PROGRESS—A COMMITTEE ON TEMPORALS—DEATH OF MR. ROBERT MENZIES—GROWTH OF LIBERALITY—THE PORTUGUESE STUDENTS—STATE OF THE MISSION—AMIABLE CHARACTER OF BISHOP GEDDES—MORALS OF EDINBURGH—DEATH OF BISHOP M'DONALD—MUCH LAMENTED—BISHOP JOHN CHISHOLM—ONLY BISHOP HAY AT HIS CONSECRATION—STUDENTS WITHHELD FROM THE MISSION—GOVERNMENT ENCOURAGES EMIGRATION—EMPLOYMENT AT GLASGOW—BANK OF SCOTLAND—BISHOP HAY INTERESTED THEREIN—THE PRIOR OF THE CARTHUSIANS THANKED—ANARCHY ADVANCING IN FRANCE—BISHOP GEDDES AT ST. OMERS ASKED TO ORDAIN—DECLINES BEING A TITULAR BISHOP "IN PART. INF:"—PROPOSED NEW CHURCH AT EDINBURGH—GLASGOW MORE LIBERAL THAN EVER—REV. ALEX. M'DONALD THERE.

During the absence of Bishop Geddes, Bishop Hay filled his place at Edinburgh ; and it was, at the time, no sinecure. The death of the much-regretted Mr. Robert Menzies, who had rendered such signal service to the Highland congregation, and the sickly state of the other priest, laid on the Bishop the whole of the parochial duty. It behooved him, also, to attend to the Procuratorship as well as his more special episcopal functions. The portions of country set apart to Bishop Geddes included Glasgow; and now, Bishop Hay, in place of his coadjutor, made a pastoral visit to that city. He remained there a week, and found the rising mission in a satisfactory condition. There had, indeed, been great progress. The change for the better that had taken place, within a few years, was truly remarkable. It remained, as yet, to appoint a permanent Incumbent. The Bishop was particularly pleased to find that there was much zeal on the part of the Catholics in contributing towards the support of a priest among them. He, accordingly, held a meeting of the more leading people and laid before them a plan for raising subscriptions. A committee of six was appointed for the management, and he provided them with a proper form of subscription papers.

Before the Bishop's return to Edinburgh, Mr. Menzies had passed away. His death was like his life, most edifying. "His loss," the Bishop wrote to Mr. Gordon, at Aberdeen, "will be severely felt in this place, as I have not one whom I can put in his place, and who has the language of his numerous congregation, without leaving an equal blank elsewhere, which, in our present circumstances, I cannot think of doing." In the same letter it is shown how liberal Edinburgh had become. "We have just such a plan for the Poor's House as you mention to be in agitation with you. But here our people who are taken in are no wise molested as to their religion, and are allowed to go to the chapel when they please; and we have free access to them in sickness. As the town of Aberdeen has always been favourable to us in this respect, I hope they will be no less so in the present case; and, if so, I much approve of what you mention, of some poor's money being applied that way, especially, as you are much better provided for that purpose than any other station I know; besides, I think it will be a real advantage in the main."

In a letter which Bishop Hay had occasion to write to Mr. Fryer, the Principal of the English College at Lisbon, concerning some Portuguese medical students, a general charge of whom the coadjutor had assumed, in compliance with the request of Her Majesty the Queen of Portugal, he gives, incidentally, a very complete account of the state of the Scotch mission at this time (1791). It was necessary to show, in connection with the charge of the students, the onerous and engrossing duties of the Vicars Apostolic. The Bishop, accordingly, writes: "We have been, for many years, and particularly at present are, in the greatest distress for the want of hands. I have at present no less than eight vacant stations, some of which are very numerous, very extended and very important. By this means we have often the great affliction to hear of poor souls dying without the sacraments, the children neglected for want of instruction, and not, unfrequently, people apostatizing for the same reason, and the neighbouring missionaries harassed and exhausted with frequent and distant calls. Three years ago, the gentleman (Rev. Andrew Dawson) who had the care of a little seminary I have for preparing boys for being sent abroad, happening to die, I had not another to put in his place, and was obliged to take that charge upon myself; otherwise I must have shut up its doors. And to this day I have not been able to get one, so that on my coming to this place I was forced to leave it to the care of servants, with the eldest of the boys to teach the younger ones their lessons. In this city we have two chapels both having pretty numerous congregations and only one clergyman to each. Bishop Geddes was obliged to assist the more important of the two, and, last Winter, from the illness of both clergymen, had for a considerable time both congregations, and for a still longer time, had one of them entirely on his hands. Although this city be his principal residence, yet, he is obliged to be out of it for weeks and often for months together several times in the year. He has to visit, from time to time, our missions in Galloway, Perthshire and Angus-shire, which I had allotted to him, having kept those in the North for my own inspection. He had the management of all the temporal affairs of the mission, and endless correspondence, both at home and abroad, relating to those affairs. He had, in fine, frequently to go to Glasgow to visit a numerous congregation there, who had no other help than from him, and, sometimes, from another living at a much greater distance from them. Such, sir, is, at present, and has been for some time past, our distressed situation, and to complete our distress, since Bishop Geddes left this, one of the two churchmen, here, is dead, which throws one of the two chapels almost entirely upon me."

For the above reasons he was averse to Bishop Geddes burdening himself with the charge of the Portuguese students, and ascribes his doing so to his disposition to do anything that was asked of him when he thought it was for the glory of God. He was also influenced by his esteem and affection for the worthy English Principal, as well as his desire to forward the views of that benevolent princess, the Queen of Portugal. The Bishop dwells at some length, on the qualities of the accomplished coadjutor: "He has certainly a most amiable temper, disinterested, obliging and condescending, and so cordially sympathizing that I know it is a torment to him to do anything harsh or severe to any mortal. This, his natural disposition, has been greatly confirmed from the example of the amiable St. Francis of Sales, whom he considers as his great model, and from the wonderful success he has had in many difficult cases by the gentle and engaging manner he treated those engaged in them. And it must be owned that this, his turn of mind, has gained him the love, esteem and regard of everyone wherever he has been, and of people of all ranks and stations who have been acquainted with him." It is to be regretted that the excellent Prelate could not give a more favourable account of the moral condition of his native town than what we find in the concluding lines of his letter to Principal Fryer : "I was born and educated in this city; and had applied to the study of medicine in my younger days before I had any knowledge of the Catholic Faith. I know what this place was at that time with regard to morals : and I am persuaded by all accounts I can get that it is, beyond any comparison, worse at present, especially in the medical line; so much so, that it is my decided opinion that it is next to a miracle if a young man, left in any degree to his own management in this vicious Sodom, and applying to the study of medicine, can ever be able to escape the contagion." This was long ago. The high reputation of the Edinburgh School of Medicine in more recent times would seem to indicate improvement.

In less than a month after the meeting at Gibston, Bishop McDonald departed this life. His health had been failing for some time, but it would appear that death came at last rather suddenly. He was much regretted by his friends and Highland flock. Their veneration for their ancient patriarchal chiefs, no doubt, added to the affection they bore to the deceased Bishop, who was a scion of the well known family of clan Ranald. The choice which he made of a coadjutor had been unanimously approved of by the clergy and laity of the Highland district, so that there was no question as to the fitness of Bishop John Chisholm to be his successor. There could be no other serious opposition than that of Mr. Chisholm himself, who was disinclined to undertake the responsibilities of so great a charge. As soon as the coadjutor crossed the border Bishop Hay was once more the only Bishop in Scotland. It fell to him, therefore, to consecrate the new Bishop, as Titular of Oria and Vicar Apostolic in the Highlands. On

February 12th the solemn rite was performed, two priests assisting, instead of Bishops, by special dispensation. At the suppression of the Jesuits, Mr. Chisholm passed from the novitiate at Tournay to the Scotch Seminary at Douai, where he was ordained priest in 1777. He had laboured happily since that time in his native district of Strathglass. He bore with honour the dignity of the mitre for more than twenty years.

It would appear that Mr. Cameron, the Principal at Valladolid, still withheld his students from the mission. This was a cause of great displeasure and vexation to Bishop Hay. It was all the more so as seven or eight stations had been vacant for several years past in the Lowland district. Now that Bishop Geddes must be absent for a time not so much as one priest could be spared, even for the Seminary. It was necessarily, therefore, placed under the charge of a young man who directed the studies of the rest. The Highland congregation sustained indeed a severe, and at the time, irreparable loss by the death of Mr. Robert Menzies who had laboured so long and so unostentatiously. The Highlanders were entirely lost for want of a priest who could speak their own tongue; and it was for some time impossible to secure such a one for the Lowland district. It would appear that the death of the most worthy Mr. Menzies was has-

tened by pecuniary anxiety. He had taken as a
boarder an Irish student of medicine, at the request
of the youth's father, and this man unfortunately,
never paid any board. The expense and vexation
thus caused, together with the liabilities of the good
priest for St. Andrew's chapel, preyed upon his mind
and brought on ague and jaundice, of which he died.

Bishop Hay, in a letter to the agent at Rome,.
gives a singularly interesting account of emigration
from the Highlands and its results as regarded the
destinies of the Glasgow mission. The letter is
dated Feb. 18th, 1792. "....Accounts have been
received from our last Summer emigrants. They
went to Nova Scotia, were kindly received, got a
year's provisions, and so much land from Government for each family. This encouragement has set
others upon following them, and we hear that subscriptions are going on for a new emigration this
year. There are many, however, of the poorer sort,
who, not being able to pay their passage, are left at
home in great misery. Would you believe it? A
door is likely to be open for them at Glasgow.
Manufacturers there are advancing to such a degree
that they cannot get hands to supply. Children of
seven years of age may make half a crown or three
shillings a week, and others more in proportion.
Application has been made to us to supply them

from the Highlands. Our only objection was the want of the exercise of their religion. This they easily saw into; and are actually concerting at present, to obviate that difficulty by providing a chapel, and have begun subscriptions among themselves to execute their plan and provide for a churchman. *Quam mirabilia sunt opera tua Domine!* If this takes place and the emigrations continue for a few years we shall have very few of our people either on the great estates of Clan Ranald or Glengary. *Dominus novit opus suum ab æterno. Fiat voluntas ejus!*"

The mission was interested in the Bank of Scotland, holding a good many shares. It was, therefore, a pleasure to the Bishop to inform his coadjutor that it was in a prosperous condition. He had recently attended a general meeting of the proprietors, at which a plan for doubling the capital was unanimously agreed to, and the bill sent to Mr. Dundas, the governor. He also mentions that, together with Bishop Chisholm and Mr. Robertson, he was at supper, for the first time, with Lord Monboddo, the good friend of Bishop Geddes, to whom he desired to he very kindly remembered. In concluding the letter he begged his coadjutor to thank the Prior of the Carthusians, in his own name and that of Bishop Chisholm, for his steady adherence to the cause of religion and of the mission, in the late negotiations at Paris. Anarchy in unfortunate France advancing every day and everything that he could have hoped to gain by his mission having been secured, Bishop Geddes left Paris for Douai, on the 20th of April. From thence he sent to the Cardinal of Propaganda a detailed account of all that he had done at Paris. The Cardinal's reply expressed approval of every step and complimented him on his success. After spending some time at Douai, he proceeded on his journey by Bruges and St. Omers. At the latter place they wished him to ordain students of the English Seminary, as the neighbouring Bishops were all absent. He had an impression, however, that titular bishops like himself, *in partibus infidelium*, were prohibited from exercising their pontifical functions beyond their own limits, even with the consent of the Ordinary. This impression Mr. Thomson subsequently confirmed by quoting the Brief that forbids it, a copy of which he sent to Bishop Geddes. War was now fairly begun between France and Austria. The day before the Bishop wrote, 10,000 men were marched from Lille to surprise Tournai. The Austrians repulsed them with great loss.

Bishop Hay, desiring to avail himself of the opportunity which his friend's journey afforded, proposed that, on his way home through England, he should recommend to their friends there, a scheme for a new church at Edinburgh. It was also still strongly urged, as formerly, by some members of the congregation. "Who knows," said the Bishop, "where a blessing may alight?" The proposed new building was intended to replace St. Margaret's only, St. Andrew's, on the east side of Blackfriar's Wynd, being still retained for the Highland congregation with services, as usual, in the Gælic language. At the time of Bishop Geddes' return to Scotland, six leading citizens of Glasgow gave Bishop Chisholm a bond for £30 a year, to Mr. Alexander McDonell, together with a free house and all that was necessary for the chapel. It gave great delight to the Catholic people of Glasgow that they were to have a resident priest; and the gentlemen who were chiefly instrumental in carrying out the arrangement, were much pleased with Mr. McDonell. This priest, afterwards so renowned in connection with Canada, had laboured hitherto in the district of Badenoch and at Fort William. The results of the liberal arrangement were highly satisfactory. It was no sooner heard of in the Highlands than twenty-four families, in all one hundred and thirty-one individuals, came to Glasgow in one day, and numbers were preparing to follow them.

Bishop Hay was anxious that his colleague of the Highlands should spare a Gælic speaking priest for Edinburgh. In the meantime Mr. A. McDonald was transferred from Drummond to St. Andrew's, Edinburgh.

CAP. XLVI.

BISHOP GEDDES PREPARES A CHINESE GRAMMAR—MANUFACTURERS OF GLASGOW PROPOSE SUBSCRIBING FOR THE ERECTION OF A CATHOLIC CHURCH—THE PENAL LAWS A HINDRANCE—THEIR ODIOUSNESS EXPOSED—CASE OF MUNSHES—THE MAGISTRATES OF DUNDEE FAVOUR A RELIEF BILL—PROPOSAL THAT THE FOUR CHIEF TOWNS SUPPORT THE SAME—BISHOP HAY WISHES TO ENLIST IN THE CAUSE BISHOP GEDDES' POWERFUL FRIENDS—MOTION LAID BEFORE PARLIAMENT—RELIEF BILL PASSED BOTH HOUSES—RECEIVED THE ROYAL SANCTION ON 3RD JUNE, 1792—NO DIRECT OPPOSITION TO THE BILL IN PARLIAMENT---A COL. M'LEOD AND LORD GEO. GORDON HOSTILE—OPPOSITION DISCOURAGED BY THE PRESS AND BY THE KIRK ASSEMBLY—THE MODERATOR THOUGHT IT NOT SUFFICIENTLY FAVOURABLE TO CATHOLICS—STATESMEN HIGHLY PLEASED—THE SUCCESSION—ANNUAL MEETING OF 1792—THANKS TO THE BISHOP OF RHODEZ—THE BISHOPS EXPRESS THEIR SYMPATHY WITH HIM IN VIEW OF THE SAD STATE OF HIS COUNTRY—REGRET FOR THE DEATH OF BISHOP M'DONALD—MRS. GOLDIE AND HER CHILDREN'S TUTORS—INTERESTING THE

NUNCIO AT LIEGE IN FAVOUR OF THE MISSION—
MUCH GOOD EXPECTED FROM BISHOP GEDDES' MIS-
SION TO PARIS—GLASGOW MANUFACTURERS PAY
THE RENT OF A LARGE HALL FOR CATHOLIC WOR-
SHIP—IMPORTANT OPENING OF THE SAME—MR.
ALEX. M'DONELL, AFTERWARDS BISHOP OF KINGS-
TON, OFFICIATING—BISHOP HAY'S OPINION OF HIM
—MAGISTRATES AND CHIEF MERCHANTS FAVOUR-
ABLE.

When Bishop Geddes reached London, on his way home, he must remain there some time in order to see friends and prepare a Chinese grammar for presentation to Mr. Dundas. In a few days it was complete; and the Bishop had a preface ready. Before it was presented Sir George Staunton, Secretary to the Embassy intended for Pekin, called in company with two missionaries from the Chinese College at Naples. In course of conversation he expressed his regret that there was no grammar of the Chinese language. The Bishop showed him the one he had prepared. He took it with him and promised to present it to Mr. Dundas.

Bishop Hay was desirous that the coadjutor before leaving London should see Mr. Dundas regarding the mission affairs of Glasgow. Some of the principal manufacturers were willing to raise a subscription towards building a church for the

Catholic people. The penal laws, however, although dormant, were still on the Statute book; and ill-disposed persons might take advantage of them to accuse those worthy gentlemen of infringing the law. Several Protestants were inclined, but for those laws, to aid in the erection of the proposed church. There occurred, meanwhile, a circumstance which proved more powerful than all the diplomacy and eloquence of Bishop Geddes. It exposed before a more enlightened public the odiousness of the penal laws. The next Protestant heir to Mr. Maxwell of Munshes, had taken measures for possessing himself of Mr. Maxwell's Annandale estate, and would, no doubt, have made good his claim but for the agitation which his proceeding occasioned among the Catholics and their friends. Bishop Hay remarked on this outrage : "It will make a curious appearance in the eyes of the world if, whilst Catholics are getting every indulgence they can reasonably desire throughout the whole British Dominions, Munshes should be deprived of such an estate merely because he is a Catholic. However, God Almighty has His own ends in view ; we must refer all to His Divine Providence, who knows how to bring good out of evil. I hope Munshes' affair in the hands of Providence will produce some good. Fiat ! Fiat !" The magistrates of Dundee had lately made an offer to

Mr. Pepper, the priest in charge there, to petition Government for the extension of the English Relief Bill to Scotland. This proposal, viewed in connection with the friendly action of the citizens of Glasgow, suggested to the Bishop a plan for obtaining the much desired relief. It was that the four leading towns in Scotland, Edinburgh, Glasgow, Aberdeen and Dundee should make a united effort in support of the good purpose. "Who knows," added the Bishop, "but Providence intends that those very places, which were lately very much against us, should be the means of befriending us? A bold stroke may be made, and sometimes succeeds best." The agent for the Crown in Edinburgh suggested to Bishop Geddes that when the Irish Relief Bill should pass, the Catholics of Scotland would do very well to bring their claims under the notice of Parliament. There was some difference of opinion as to the extent of what should be asked for. Bishop Hay inclined for a general repeal of disabilities rather than of those only which affected the power of Catholics to hold property. His views were expressed at some length in a letter to the coadjutor. He considered the time exceedingly favourable, and continuing said : "If Mr. Constable gets any motion made for securing our property would it not be proper for you to write to Lord Gower before it come in, to see if he could get any of his friends to move for the extension of the English Bill to Scotland ? Could you not suggest it, also, to Mr. Secretary Dundas ? * * * The general run of the country is in our favour, and I do not think that your using your influence with your great friends could do any harm. If matters were carried through at once there could not be the least danger ; but if property alone were sought and obtained they might raise a splutter (if they were inclined to make one) to prevent our getting more, of which property would be considered as a prelude. This was the rock our friend split upon when the first application was made. Had Scotland been included in the first Bill there would have probably been no disturbance. And, from the experience of what happened then, I am fully persuaded that it would be much easier to get the whole at once, just now, than to get a part now and the rest hereafter. Might you not, at least suggest these reflections to Mr. Constable, as well as to your other friends ?" * * In a second letter on the subject, the Bishop earnestly urged on his coadjutor the propriety of communicating with his powerful friends, and expressed anew his conviction that the most complete relief should be asked for. He addressed, moreover, a circular letter to the Catholic proprietors, inviting their co-operation with Munshes, and proposing, as the most

expeditious and economical plan, the simple extension
of the English Bills of Relief to Scotland. "We cannot expect, nor would I desire more; and if we got it, it would make us very easy." Mr. Menzies, of Pitfodels, was associated with Munshes and Mr. Constable in bringing the matter before Parliament. The Lord Advocate, on April 22nd, moved for leave to bring in a Bill to relieve the Scotch Roman Catholics from certain penalties and disabilities imposed on them by former Acts of the Scotch Parliament, and especially in the eighth and ninth sessions of the first Parliament of King William. The preamble of the Bill asserted that former acts of repression had been deemed expedient as chiefly directed against persons who acknowledged, or were supposed to acknowledge, the temporal superiority or power of the Pope over Scotland; an opinion contrary to the allegiance of the subjects of that kingdom. The preamble to the new Bill further declared that the *formula* hitherto imposed on the Roman Catholics of Scotland amounted only to a renunciation of speculative and dogmatic opinions. It was, therefore, enacted that, from this date, the Scotch Roman Catholics who should take and subscribe the oath of abjuration and the declaration annexed to the Bill should be exempted from all the pains, penalties and disabilities

imposed, enacted, revived, ratified and confirmed by the said Act of the eighth and ninth sessions of the first Parliament of King William III, as fully and effectually as if such persons had actually made the renunciation of Popery thereby ordained, according to the formula thereunto subjoined. A certain amount of legal shuffling and quibbling was but a small price to pay for so important a measure of justice to the Catholics of Scotland. The formula was declared to have been aimed at persons who held political doctrines inconsistent with the duties of good British subjects. Yet the formula was also declared to comprehend only religious opinions, and to be, therefore, imperative as regarded political opinions. For which reason the new Act of Relief proposed to substitute a more efficient check to political heresy, under cover of which the offensive formula was set aside as inefficient; and thus a measure of religious liberty was secured for the Roman Catholics in Scotland. The Bill was read a first time, April 25th, and its provisions were even more favourable than the Catholics themselves had hoped for. The Oath subjoined was the same as that prescribed by the last English Relief Act, and was one against which no scruple could exist. By taking it a Catholic was fully enabled to acquire, possess and dispose of his real and personal estate in Scotland, as any other subject could. An exception, however, was retained which forbade any Catholic, even after taking the Oath, from discharging the office of a governor, pedagogue, teacher, tutor or curator, chamberlain or factor, to any child or children of Protestant parents ; neither could he be employed in their education or in the trust and management of their affairs. The Bill prohibited a Catholic from being a schoolmaster, professor or public teacher of any science in Scotland. Notwithstanding these drawbacks the Bill was thankfully received by the Catholic body ; Bishop Hay's only disparaging remark being that the exception about teaching was rather inconvenient. The Bill passed the Upper House on May 24th, and received the Royal Assent on June 3rd. Bishop Geddes, in communicating this good news to Bishop Hay, sincerely congratulated him upon it, and expressed his hope that the Bishop might live many years to see the good effects resulting from this favour of Providence. He writes also some very interesting particulars illustrative of the history of the Bill: "The first sketch of the Bill which was concerted in Scotland would have excluded converts from all benefit of the Act, and had a clause declaring illegal all donations to religious societies. But these odious parts were cut out by the present and late chancellors."

There was not the least direct opposition made to us in either House of Parliament; but, it is suspected that Colonel McLeod and the Duke of Norfolk, by proposing to give up more privileges, intended to create delays, and even, perhaps, to raise discontent in Scotland. It seems Lord George Gordon also bestirred himself; but there has scarcely been a murmur that I have heard, which, I believe, owing greatly to the quiet manner in which the affair has been gone about and the very obliging disposition of the publishers of our newspapers who unanimously agreed to reject every inflammatory composition that was offered them for publication. There was no mention made of us in the general Assembly. Its Moderator, Dr. Hardie, had seen the Bill at London and had said that it was not favourable enough to us. The Lord Advocate has behaved extremely well; and, last week when I thanked him, he seemed happy at what he had done, and assured me the exceptions had been left merely for peace's sake but that they will never be minded. We meet with many congratulations; but none seems to be more glad at this event than your friends, Mr. Arbuthnot and Andrew Stewart (Protestants.) Mr. Maxwell, of Munshes, is returned home in very good spirits, and has brought another emigrant priest along with him. He and Mr. Constable have paid the expenses in the first instance and will not, I believe, be very rigourous in exacting repayment; but Mr. Menzies, of Pitfodels, from whom I heard yesterday from Tunbridge Wells, is strongly of opinion that all proprietors should contribute proportionally, and has written to that purpose to Kirkconnell.

You will, I am persuaded, think his proposal reasonable; and the sum is, I believe, very moderate. Lord Kelly was the mover in the House of Lords, and expressed great satisfaction in having been so, when he lately dined with Mr. Arbuthnot, where Mr. McPherson also was. With regard to the Act itself it almost puts an end to the penal laws against us, as the exceptions are so few and trifling, and purposely there is no penalty annexed to them. Besides the English Catholics have it in contemplation to apply soon for being put entirely on the same footing with other subjects; and when that happens we may now reasonably hope to be included with them."

The clause in the Oath regarding the Protestant succession appeared at one time to Bishop Geddes to be objectionable. On further consideration, however, his view changed. That succession was confirmed by law, ingrafted in the Constitution. More, it was necessary, he considered, for the national tranquility. He submitted to it, therefore, and could safely promise to maintain it as long as it should continue to be the law of the land and part and parcel of the Constitution. "Every prudent person amongst us," he writes, "will see how proper it is for us not to appear elevated on this occasion, so as to give any offence to Protestants, and this behaviour, you (Bishop Hay) will, no doubt, recommend."

The Bishops held their annual meeting in July this year, 1792, at Scalan. Their usual letters to Rome were then prepared; and in addition they despatched a joint letter to the Prior of the Carthusians and the arbiters in the recent conference at Paris, cordially thanking them for their services. To the excellent Bishop of Rhodez, also they expressed their gratitude for the interest which he had kindly taken in the Scotch College, and the laborious services which he had rendered to it, particularly by his communication to the Principal. They requested that he would still obligingly continue to watch over the affairs of the College. They concluded by expressing very feelingly their sympathy with him in the distressed condition of his country, confidently hoping that in the ways of Providence a vineyard once so flourishing would be restored to its former splendour, and their highly valued friend, the Bishop, to the undisturbed charge of his beloved flock.

In their letter to Cardinal Antonelli and Propaganda the Bishops intimated the recent death of their colleague of the Highland district, Bishop Alexander Macdonald, describing him as "a pious and devoted prelate," and a descendant of the ancient family of Clan Ranald. They also mentioned, and with honour, Mrs. Goldie, a convert, who, rather than allow her children to be brought up as Protestants, put to sea in most unfavourable weather, together with her son of seven and her daughter of eleven years of age; and without previously giving notice to her friends, sought a home in the convent of English Nuns at Rouen, confining herself to the care of God's Providence. It is so far to the credit of the children's tutors that they did not proceed to extreme measures, but supplied the family with money.

In compliance with the request of the Nuncio at Liege, Bishop Hay wrote to him some details of the state of the mission, not forgetting to suggest that it would be acceptable and meritorious on the part of His Excellency to interest himself in its favour. The Bishops before separating, expressed their satisfaction with the results of Bishop Geddes' mission to Paris. They hoped to derive from it much permanent good whatever might be the state of public affairs in France.

Meanwhile, it gave them pleasure to hear of Mr. Alex. McDonell's success at Glasgow, A very large hall was hired there from the Duke of Hamilton and the Lord Provost, for the purpose, as was well known, of a Catholic chapel. The principal manufacturers placed seats in it for 300 persons, and became security for the rent, £40. The town clerk showed his friendship, as did also the Board of Trade and a society for preventing emigration. Acting thus liberally, they could have had no surer means of securing sober and industrious men for their employment. The opening of the chapel on 21st October, made an epoch in the history of the Glasgow mission. The congregation that assembled on the occasion amounted to over two hundred. Mr. McDonell officiated in the new chapel for the first time. This was welcome news to Bishop Hay; and yet his remembrance of former things caused him to have some misgiving. Mr. McDonell's hopes were raised so high and his ambition so much excited that the cautious Bishop could not help being "much afraid that he had a little touch of the common turn (*perfervidum ingenium scotorum*, propably,) too prevalent amongst us." This, however, was but the passing thought of the moment ; for, a few days later, he bore high testimony to the fine qualities of the Glasgow missionary. "Mr. McDonell," he writes to Bishop Geddes, Dec. 17th, "is of a forward and intrepid disposition ; but I have often seen that when Providence has a mind to bring about any event He qualifies the instrument He makes use of for that purpose ; and very often a certain degree of boldness produces much better effects than too much timidity. I trust in God that will be the case with our friend there." So far the Glasgow mission was prosperous and promising. The magistrates and principal merchants were highly favourable ; and, moreover, the associations that were arising and causing alarm to the Government, held "liberty to the Papists," as part and parcel of their reform.

CAP. XLVII.

PRINCIPLES OF THE FRENCH REVOLUTION IN SCOTLAND—OFFENDERS IMPRISONED—TREE OF LIBERTY AT DUNDEE—RIOTING—DRAGOONS REQUIRED TO RESTORE ORDER—DECLINING HEALTH OF BISHOP GEDDES—BAD PRINCIPLES OF THE TIMES DISCUSSED—STATESMEN FRIENDLY TO CATHOLICS—PRINCE ERNEST AUGUSTUS AT PROPAGANDA—ENGLISH IN FAVOUR AT ROME—AN AMBASSADOR FROM ROME TO LONDON—REV. PAUL MACPHERSON, AGENT AT ROME, ON THE DEATH OF MR. THOMSON—END OF DOUAI COLLEGE—BISHOP GEDDES AT SCALAN—IMPORTANCE OF MISSION HISTORY—ALEXANDER PATERSON AT GLENLIVAT—BISHOP HAY PROCURATOR AT EDINBURGH—THE BISHOP OF THE HIGHLANDS ILL—ONLY TWO BISHOPS AT ANNUAL MEETING—THEY INFORM ROME OF RELIEF BILL, AND SUBSCRIBE OATH OF ALLEGIANCE—WONDERFUL CHANGE OF PUBLIC FEELING ASCRIBED TO BISHOP GEDDES.

The principles of French politics were spreading at this time in Scotland. In France what they called a constitutional government was exercising despotism over public opinion. Associations or clubs for the diffusion of revolutionary opinions began to make themselves be felt at Edinburgh. In November, they published certain resolutions. To their just demands for Government reform they, with the want of tact and prudence incident to nearly every popular movement, united in an absurd protest against one man's having the right to the obedience of another, together with other revolutionary tenets of the French school. It was said that two-thirds of the citizens of the capital favoured those opinions. Two papers were published weekly as their organs. The streets echoed at night with cries of "No King! No aristocrats!" Some of the more audacious partizans attempted to fraternize with the soldiers in the castle, treating them to drink and promising every man among them 1s. 6d. a day, if he would join the clubs. Information of these reckless proceedings led to the apprehension and imprisonment of the offenders in the tolbooth or jail of Edinburgh, a prison which the great novelist has since immortalized under its romantic name of "The Heart of Mid Lothian." On the same day the tree of liberty was planted at the market cross of Dundee. A gentleman of effervescent loyalty, who pulled it down, had his windows broken and his manufactory entirely demolished. The magistrates were driven from the town, and the assistance of the dragoons was necessary to restore order. It is not a little noticeable that the injustice suffered by the British Catholics was put prominently forward by all these revolutionary clubs as a grievous wrong, calling for sympathy and redress. As in man's constitution, so in that of a nation, a weak point is certainly detected in a crisis of general infirmity.

To the great regret of the Catholic people the health of Bishop Geddes was now declining rapidly. His toilsome journey to Orkney had injured him, and the fatigue incident to his negotiations at Paris gave a second shock to his constitution. Rheumatism now seized on his limbs, and he could neither walk nor travel on horseback. The most eminent physicians of the time, Doctors Gregory and Spens, were consulted. They prescribed, among other things, rest; and he retired to Leith, which was not then the busy seaport it has since become. He could only write with difficulty and slowly. For the most part he employed an amanuensis; and the Rev. Paul McPherson, before his appointment to the Roman agency, generally performed this office. Neither rest nor medicine appeared to do any good; and a form of paralysis began to be felt. His illness caused great concern to Bishop Hay; and he often and feelingly expressed it.

The Bishops conceived the idea of publishing a pastoral letter on the subject of the seditious spirit that was showing itself in the country ; and, indeed, not unadvisedly. Lord Adam Gordon, the commander in chief, had requested Bishop Geddes to speak on the subject to his people in church. The proposal gave rise to some discussion. There was even doubt in the Bishop's mind whether the pastoral should be published at all. The Lord Advocate and the agent for the Crown were consulted. These gentlemen appeared to fear lest its publication might be attended with some danger, and might excite ill-will against Catholics, in the agitated state of the public mind. Bishop Geddes, to whom Bishop Hay left the decision of the matter, thought himself that such a result was not improbable ; and, therefore, the publication of the pastoral was abandoned. The proposal to issue a pastoral letter in the cause of order, together with the discussions and consultations to which it led, failed not to increase the favour with which the Bishops were looked upon by the men in power.

A circumstance may here be mentioned which shows how popular the British were at Rome. Mr. Peter McLachlan, a Scotch student at Rome, wrote to Bishop Hay under date of 14th January, 1798, that Prince Ernest Augustus, the King's son, had been in Rome about two months and intended to stay till the end of April. He came one day to the Academy of Languages at Propaganda, where he was treated with as much respect and distinction as they could have shown to the Pope himself, the hall being most superbly hung with rich tapestry and a throne erected for him in the middle. On leaving Propaganda he received a popular ovation. As soon as he was recognized the people flocked around him and began to cry out "*Viva il Re e la familia Reale d inghilterra! Viva l'inghilterra! Viva il Papa ed Inghilterra!*" and could by no means, be prevailed on to depart until they had kissed his hand, as was the custom in Italy. Such was the reputation England had gained by reason of the decent and becoming behaviour of the English who resorted to Rome in vast numbers.

Mr. Thomson, the agent of the mission at Rome, having died, it became necessary to appoint a successor. It was difficult to part with any of the priests, who were so few in number; and yet so much depended on the Roman Agency, that some one must be spared. The business of the mission must be attended to, and particularly that which regarded the Scotch College. Mr. Smelt, the agent of the English clergy, was requested to act in the meantime. And now came a rumour that a representative of the Holy See was on his way to London in order to solicit the aid of England against the French. Bishop Hay, on hearing this news, expressed not his surprise, but rather that he was not surprised. "An ambassador of any kind from Hillton (the city of the seven hills) to London is, indeed, an extraordinary phenomenon! But how can we be surprised at any thing in this age of wonders!" Surprised or not surprised, the Bishop was resolved to avail himself of the circumstance for a good purpose. If the mission from Rome succeeded Mr. Henry Dundass, the friend of the Bishops, would, perhaps, request of the Holy Father as a favour to his British allies, the appointment of a national president to the Scotch College. Strong reasons might be urged in support of the minister's interference.

After some consultation with Bishop Chisholm, the Rev. Paul Macpherson was appointed to the Roman agency. There was only one objection, his great usefulness as Procurator of the mission. He was himself much inclined to the appointment, He had for some time considered that it would be his greatest happiness to live at Rome, He now had his wish; and it came in a way that could not but be pleasing to him.

The Scotch College at Douai, as had been feared for some time, had now reached the "beginning of the end." It was narrowly watched and the public seals placed on its property. It was left to Mr. Farquarson, who possessed the full confidence of the Bishops, to do the best that could be done in the circumstances. His chief care was to send home the students ; and it was arranged that they should travel under the charge of Mr. Alexander Paterson. It was appointed that some of them should study at Valladolid and others at home. One of them, Mr. Andrew Scott, who had just commenced the study of divinity, was assigned as a companion to Mr. Andrew Carruthers at Scalan. The students reached London in safety. Thence they took ship for Berwick, and were at Edinburgh by the middle of April. The names of some of the students for the Lowlands will be long remembered in that country. They are Andrew Scott, afterwards Bishop, William McDonald, William Wallace, James Paterson, William Smith, and Alexander Badenoch.

The time was now come when the increasing illness of Bishop Geddes required that he should have complete exemption from care and labour. This he could not enjoy at Edinburgh. Retiring to Leith was only like taking an airing next door. His cares, if not all the fatigue of duty, followed him. It was finally resolved, after much deliberation, that he should reside at Scalan, Bishop Hay taking his place at Edinburgh. His presence at the Seminary would be useful without requiring any exertion on his part. Mr. Andrew Carruthers being charged with the harder duties. He would not, however, be altogether idle, as he hoped, with the aid of an amanuensis, to do something towards forwarding his proposed work, the History of the Scotch Missions, which he had long had much at heart. The importance of such a history was becoming greater every day and at no time was it more important than at that in which he lived. The perfect quiet of Scalan and its pure mountain air must have been highly favourable to the invalid. But his illness was beyond remedy. So thought Bishop Hay, an excellent judge. The Bishop knew to whom he was writing, when he said, in a letter to the patient: "With regard to my opinion about your health, I always considered your case to be of the paralytical kind, at least since the full accounts you gave me of it, I think at our last Gibston meeting, and I honestly own to you, my most dear sir, with that candour which I owe to you as a real friend, that I have no great expectations of a thorough recovery, at least of a speedy one, whatever, the doctors may say. I have known people even of a considerable age, who, after a sudden and even severe fit of palsy, have recovered beyond expectation, but when it begins, in a manner insensibly, as yours did, and advances almost by imperceptible degrees, to the length yours has come, I own I see little ground to expect what we so earnestly wish for."

Bishop Geddes, with the hope of seeing something done towards preparing a history of the Scotch mission, proposed to carry with him to Scalan, a collection of old letters that were in his possession, out of which he would extract at his leisure, whatever information they might contain relating to the mission. The more he gave his attention to this subjuct the more important it appeared to him. A knowledge of mission history, he was confident, would have prevented many disputes. Bishop Hay had no objection to this study, except on account of its demand on his strength, the little application it required being beyond his powers and contrary to what his physicians advised.

Having appointed Mr. Paterson, "a very sensible and well principled young man," (and afterwards so good a Bishop), to the mission of Glenlivat, Bishop Hay, on the 8th of June, 1793, bade adieu once more to his favourite retreat at Scalan. He named Mr. James Sharp as his assistant in the mission duty of Edinburgh. He himself undertook to fill the office of Procurator at least for a year.

The Bishop of the Highland district being detained at home by illness, the two Bishops of the Lowlands only attended the annual meeting. In their usual letter to Rome they had the satisfaction to inform Cardinal Antonelli and Propaganda of the repeal of the penal laws. They also communicated directly this acceptable intelligence to the Holy Father, and besought him at the same time to use his authority in reforming the condition of the Scotch College at Rome. The first important act of Bishop Hay at Edinburgh on his return from Scalan and the last of his invalid coadjutor, was to take and subscribe the Oath of Allegiance required by the recent Relief Bill. Both Bishops appeared before the Sheriff substitute of Midlothian, swore aud subscribed as required.

The invaluable work of Bishop Geddes at the capital was now at an end. His amiability and various accomplishments, his distinguished literary merit and eminent virtue had won for him many friends in every religious denomination. He beheld in his time that extraordinary revolution in public feeling which resulted in the unanimous passing of the Relief Bill ; and this revolution was due in great measure to his personal influence. Men of the highest reputation, lawyers, judges, men of letters, learned to respect his religion in respecting the man who professed it, and in whom they recognized their equal in intellectual power and acquirement, whilst they found him genial as he was gifted. The mind of Bishop Hay, though possibly more vigourous and profound, was not so versatile; and he was certainly not adapted, although possessed of many accomplishments, to shine in general society. People revered him, nevertheless; but they loved the coadjutor. Catholics, both clergy and laity, were irresistibly under the influence of like feelings. How sorrowful, then, must not have been the parting with such a Bishop, and for such a cause!

CAP. XLVIII.

BENEFIT OF RELIEF—BISHOP HAY AT EDINBURGH—SICK SOLDIERS DESIRING TO BE CATHOLICS—THE DUKE OF GORDON AT SCALAN—A BRITISH FLEET DEFENDS THE ROMAN COURT—DESIRE FOR A NATIONAL RECTOR—MR. MACPHERSON SPECIALLY RECOMMENDED TO THE CARDINAL, DUKE OF YORK—PAOLI—BRITISH EXPECTED ON ROMAN COAST—THE STUDENTS FROM DOUAI—THE SCOTCH CATHOLICS FAVOURED IN ENGLAND—THE "LAND OF CAKES"—GEORGE CHALMERS—MR. ALEX. PATERSON ACCOUNTS FOR DISCONTENT IN SCOTLAND—MR. JAMES PATERSON—FIFTEEN THOUSAND EMIGRANTS—FRENCH CLERGY IN LONDON—GREATEST RESPECT SHOWN THEM—THE CONTRARY AT BRUGES—THE BRITISH GOVERNMENT GIVES FREE PASSAGE TO EXILED CLERGY TO ENGLAND—SAILORS EXPRESS THEIR SYMPATHY—REVOLUTIONARY EMISSARIES PROMOTE HATRED OF THE BRITISH—BISHOP HAY ON THE DIFFICULTY AT SCALAN—EXTRAORDINARY IGNORANCE AT THE TWO SCOTCH MONASTERIES IN BAVARIA—DESIRE TO HAVE THEM CONVERTED INTO COLLEGES.—

The Bishops now issued a pastoral letter acknowledging the eminent services of our public men and the better feeling of the people in passing the Relief Bill. Referring to the repealed laws as they once stood against Catholics, it observed : "Those times, blessed be God! are now no more. Our humane and generous legislators, after being fully satisfied as to the innocence of our tenets, the purity of our moral doctrine, our attachment to the Government, and our love to the happy constitution of our country, have, with the greatest unanimity and approbation of both houses of Parliament, repealed the penal laws that stood against us and extended to us, the Catholics of this country, the favour lately granted to those of England and Ireland, by which we may now enjoy the free and undisturbed exercise of our holy religion." The faithful were then called upon to return thanks to Almighty God for His recent goodness to them. To Him they owed the humane disposition of their rulers; to Him the acquiescence of the whole nation in what their rulers had done for them. To gratitude they were bound to join a sincere repentance for their own sins and the sins of their forefathers which had provoked the Divine anger against them. As to their earthly rulers Catholics were bound to pray for them, and to show, on all occasions, a high respect for, and a strict obedience to the laws, as faithful subiects of His Majesty, as good citizens and worthy members of society. The Bishops, in conclusion, besought the Catholic body to use their recovered liberty with prudence and moderation, so as by their quiet and peaceable demeanour, to convince the world that they were not unworthy of the favour lately bestowed on them. The pastoral letter presented an admirable model of temperate and chastened expression. It was dated July 12th, 1793.

Bishop Hay now resumed the duty of the principal charge of the congregation at Edinburgh, with Mr. James Sharp for his assistant. He went to reside in the house underneath St. Margaret's chapel, where his name, Mr. Hay, in faded paint, might have been seen, not long ago, and may still, perhaps, be seen, on the strong outer door of the house, opening on the third floor of the common stair. Mr. James Sharp, when on his way to Scotland, found Mr. Oliver at Ostend, on a mission of charity to some sick soldiers of the 27th Regiment. Some of them desired to become Catholics. "*Spiritus ubi vult spirat.*"

Bishop Geddes on arriving at Scalan found the community there in good health, and under the temporary charge of Mr. Andrew Carruthers. The Duke of Gordon had paid a visit to the Seminary the week before, and had expressed himself satisfied with the condition of the place. Bishop

Geddes availed himself of the Duke's visit to say that he hoped His Grace would give them a long lease, as a good deal of money had been laid out on the establishment. The Duke replied that they should not differ. The Douai students, recently placed in the Seminary were discontented, and gave trouble. They complained of the beds, of the food, of the untidiness of their companions, etc.

As has been seen, the Court of Rome had expressed a desire for the protection of the British Government against the French. The request was now renewed through Bishop Douglas, as the states of the Church were seriously threatened by France. In compliance with the application presented by Bishop Douglas, Lord Hood's fleet was sent to defend the Roman Court. It appeared to be a favourable opportunity for insisting on having national superiors in charge of the British Colleges. Bishop Douglas, if necessary, would induce Lord Grenville to support the measure.

The Rev. Paul McPherson was now taking leave of his friends and preparing for his journey to Rome. Bishop Hay provided him with letters of introduction to numerous influential parties in the Holy City. He addressed, in his favour, with special recommendations, Cardinals Antonelli, Albani, Caraffa, Trajetto and Borgia, who was recently created a cardinal. The Bishop, still more particularly, solicited for the agent the good will of the Cardinal, Duke of York. In his letter of introduction, he reminded the Cardinal of their friendly relations in 1782, when His Eminence expressed the desire that the Bishop should write to him when the affairs of the mission required it, *tanquam Episcopus ad Episcopum.* It was this expression of the Cardinal's goodness which encouraged him to recommend Mr. McPherson, in a special manner, to his protection. The Bishop, moreover, prayed His Eminence to obtain for him from the Dataria, the pension enjoyed by the last two agents.

In July the Romans were anxiously looking for the arrival on their coast of the British Fleet. Spanish ships of war were cruising in considerable force, between Genoa and Corsica, in order to prevent the landing of French troops on the Island. General Paoli was in the field at the head of a considerable force. He had declared his independence, and was only waiting, it was understood, for the arrival of the British fleet to make himself master of the whole Island.

The students who had come from Douai were now an occasion of some difficulty. They could not remain at Scalan. After some discussion it was decided that they should be sent to prosecute their studies at Valladolid with the exception of two, Alexander Badenoch, who retired to his family until his health should be confirmed, and Andrew Scott, for whom, as he was truly pious and could be depended on, it was appointed that he should stay with Bishop Hay at Edinburgh. It would appear that the boy, Andrew Scott, was in delicate health, it being mentioned that his stay at Edinburgh would prove beneficial, as it gave him the opportunity of drinking the water of St. Bernard's well.

The Catholics of Scotland appear to have been in high favour with their brethren in England. Mr. McPherson when in London on his way to Rome, dined one day together with Bishop Douglas, with two hundred members and benefactors of a charitable institution, who drank to the health of Bishops Hay and Geddes, not forgetting to honour the national toast "the land of cakes." Mr. McPherson met with much civility and kindness on the part of Bishop Douglas, whose goodness and piety he admired more than his abilities. Some among the clergy and the Catholic laity caused the good Bishop a great deal of trouble. "In comparison with these," writes Mr. McPherson, "the most refractory subjects in Scotland were as lambs."

Mr. George Chalmers, also, having received Bishop Geddes' letter of introduction, gave a cordial welcome to Mr. McPherson, who wrote about him afterwards, as an accomplished scholar and, in the full sense of the word, a gentleman. Mr. Chalmers was a true friend to the Scotch Catholics, and as, from his acquaintance with many leading statesmen, he professed great influence, he proposed recommending the matter of placing national superiors over the colleges at Rome, to Mr. Dundas, and through him to Lord Grenville. The distinguished author of "Caledonia" could not have more effectually shown his good will. Bishop Douglas, on the contrary, when consulted, showed himself jealous of Bishop Hay or any one else but himself, interfering with the question of national superiors. The Bishop of Rhodez being in London, on his way to Scotland, honoured Mr. McPherson with several letters of introduction; among the rest, one to Cardinal Bernis.

Mr. Alexander Paterson, the priest of Glenlivat, in giving a full account to Bishop Hay of the discontent of the Douai students at Scalan, makes allowance for the great change in their food and studies, but thinks that if the Bishop had remained there would have heen no complaint. He lays all the blame on the youth in whose charge they were left. "A young man." he writes, "in entering on a new charge, ought to be extremely cautious and circumspect in showing his authority. This precaution, I believe, Mr. Carruthers was not careful enough to take. He had to deal with his former companions, his own school-fellows, his most intimate friends. Too overbearing a disposition with regard to some, gained him the disaffection of all. One thing brought on another, and Scalan became disgustful. To be sure, they ought to have behaved otherwise than they did. But methods must be sometimes contrived to make them do from inclination what they are obliged to do from duty. I know Mr. Carruthers to be a lad of solid piety, much good sense, and not ordinary abilities; but, whilst *in other things I commend him, in this* (the college matter) *I do not commend him.*" The worthy farmer at Scalan was resolved to leave it. On Mr. Paterson asking him his reason, he replied that Mr. Carruthers found fault with his work, and did not seem to care that he should go back after being ill some time, but engaged another man, whom he shortly dismissed without paying his wages, because he had been absent for a day or two on his own farm. If And. Carruthers went on in that way not a lad in the country would come near Scalan. Mr. Paterson, who knew the worth of the good servant, advised him to consider Bishop Hay's interest. He acknowledged the Bishop's kindness and said there was not one in the world whom he would like better to serve; but he could not and would not be "bully-ragged" while he was able to earn his bread more peaceably and advantageously elsewhere. The good housekeeper, whose services the venerable Bishop highly appreciated, was thinking of leaving on account of Mr. Carruthers' treatment of her. Mr. Alexander Paterson's conclusion was that Mr. Carruthers should be immediately superseded, and Mr. James Paterson put in his place. This young man, indeed, was only a student, but happily he understood the art of teaching others; and he was feared and loved, at the same time, by the younger boys under his charge. All this Mr. Paterson could bear witness to from his former knowledge of him.

Mr. McPherson on reaching Bruges, wrote to Bishop Geddes, informing him of some additional incidents of his journey. He expressed great surprise at the attention shown to the French emigrant clergy in London. There were about 1,500 of them there. The same was the case at Dover. So many of them were met in the streets there that one might conclude the town was half filled with French priests. Every one paid them great respect; whilst, on the other hand, at Bruges, where he was writing, they could hardly appear in the streets without being hissed. "Generous Britain!" exclaimed the agent, "Heaven must reward such eminent charity." Not a farthing was exacted from the French priests passing between Dover and Ostend. The British Government provided for their fare : and, English passengers, when there were any, paid for their food. If there were none, the brave tars would say :—and, what they said is best given in their own language.—" D——n their eyes, would they allow a poor French priest to pay for a meal or two?" This homely utterance shows how widespread, wherever there were Englishmen, on land or at sea, was the sympathy of the British people with the victims of a revolution unparalleled in its atrocity. The agent then gives an account of the escape of the Principal and some students from the Scotch College at Douai. He concludes his letter by remarking that the majority of the French people were friendly to the English; but that revolutionary emissaries with the malignity of demons, were doing everything in their power to exasperate them against British subjects.

Bishop Hay found it to be necessary to write to Mr. Andrew Carruthers, plainly telling him his mind as regarded the trouble at Scalan. But it was not an easy matter to make the young man sensible of his errors. The Bishop had ascribed to his "harshness and severity" the misconduct of some of the seminary and the discontent of all the rest. Mr. Carruthers defended himself ingeniously, but in that forbiddingly affected and pompous style which was then habitual to him. The Bishop, moreover, had condemned him for giving his opinion so freely about the servants. In regard to this matter he wisely promised to do better for the future. But his tone is full of consequence, as if he were waiving a right for the public good. This affair and others he discussed with the Bishop, with the air of a man who was debating with an equal, and who was, in fact, the aggrieved and nobly forgiving opponent of the Bishop and of every one at Scalan. All this is written with the utmost reluctance. It would please the writer more to dwell, and dwell only, on Mr. Carruthers' devoted and unremitting attention to the invalid Bishop; but inexorable history requires, above all things, that the truth be told.

It was desirable, considering the alienation of the colleges in France, that subjects for the mission should be obtained from the Scotch Monastery at Ratisbon. But such was the state of that House that anything of the kind was out of the question. Mr. Macpherson, on arriving at Ratisbon, found that the two Scotch convents in Bavaria maintained very dangerous principles. Ignorance, he stated, was the cause. One of the Scotch monks seriously assured him that St. Augustine wrote all his works in Greek. Another, a few minutes afterwards, said that throughout all the saint's writings, the Manichean heresy was clear, and that certainly he never knew a word of Greek. They conversed only about gambling, hunting, and a kind of politics. He would be sorry to hear of one of them being in the mission.' Notwithstanding, he was kindly entertained in both the monasteries. It was quite different at the English academy of Liege. There, the good old maxims prevailed. There, also, he was hospitably entertained. The remedy, Bishop Hay conceived, for the bad state of matters at Ratisbon was to have the monastery converted into a college; and an excellent ground for proceeding on was the impossibility of finding subjects for the monastery. The monks must all be natives of Scotland; and how could Scotland supply such persons now that it was so generally Protestantized? Now that the national colleges in France were lost, it would be an irreparable loss to religion in Scotland, if Ratisbon and Wirtzburgh were nullified for want of subjects.

CAP. XLIX.

BISHOP GEDDES ILL AT ABERDEEN—CONTRIBUTES TO THE ENCYCLOPEDIA BRITANNICA — DR. GLEIG— MR. JAMES SHARPE AT SCALAN—PROPAGANDA ON RELIEF BILL — SCOTCH MISSION HIGHLY CONSIDERED AT ROME—DEATH OF MUNSHES—PRIESTS NOT REMOVED—MISS RIDDELL'S BEQUEST—MGR. ERSKINE'S INFLUENCE IN FAVOUR OF THE MISSION —BISHOP GEDDES ABLE TO DO LITERARY WORK —REPORT TO ROME—POPULAR PREJUDICE MUCH DIMINISHED— NUMBER OF CATHOLICS — EMIGRATION TO AMERICA—RESOURCES OF THE MISSION —INEFFICIENCY OF THE SCOTCH MONASTERIES IN GERMANY—THE CATHOLICS APPLY FOR INFORMATION REGARDING THEIR NEWLY ACQUIRED LIBERTIES — BANNS IN " PARISH CHURCH " — WHETHER THE KIRK'S CENSURES WERE TO BE SUBMITTED TO—LIBERTY IN REGARD TO BAPTISM —DUES PAYABLE TO SESSION CLERK AND BEADLE.

Bishop Geddes' illness increasing with redoubled severity, and, winter approaching, it was thought that he would be less uncomfortable at Aberdeen. The priest there, Mr. Gordon, was his nephew, and kindly invited him to his house. He removed, accordingly, with as little fatigue as possible, to the northern city, the climate of which was considered favourable to invalids, and which, indeed, had proved so in the case of Bishop Grant. It was a cause of great distress to Bishop Geddes that he was no longer able to apply to the literary labour that was necessary for completing his history of the Scotch mission.

The invalid Bishop had bestowed his services in connection with the *Encyclopedia Britannica*, of which Dr. George Gleig, Episcopalian minister of Stirling, was the editor. His first contribution to this publication was on the subject of the Pope. Dr. Gleig wrote a friendly letter, free of all pedantry and affectation, addressing *Right Revd. Mr. Geddes,* Aberdeen, to thank the Bishop and compliment him on the candour of his paper, and on its interesting information, especially about the election of the Pope. He asked him, moreover, for a reference to one or two standard Catholic works on the Papal supremacy for insertion at the end of the article. He also suggested difficulties regarding the deposing power, not, he said, for captiousness, but to remove plausible objections to what the contemplated article on that subject would advance. He much regretted the state of the Bishop's health, which he feared, the dreadful news from France would tend to aggravate. Dr. Gleig concluded by desiring that the Bishop would send him any suggestions about the Encyclopedia, which might divert his mind from his sufferings, and which would be thankfully received by the editor.

It was now appointed that Mr. Alexander Paterson should receive into his house of Cean-na-Coille beside his chapel, Charles Gordon and James Paterson, two of the students who had escaped from Douai and were studying their courses of philosophy. Mr. James Sharp was destined to supersede Mr. Carruthers at Scalan. There was some difficulty, however, in getting the latter to leave the Seminary. He still indulged in the same lofty tone of equality when discussing matters with his superiors. Peace and unity, however, required that he should no longer hold office at the Seminary. Mr. Paterson appears to have got tired of him very soon ; for we find that he proposed to exchange Mr. Carruthers for the Bishop's boarder, Andrew Scott, a youth who would be more easily satisfied with his clothing, and would, also, be no less useful than Mr. Carruthers in every way. Mr. Paterson was allowed £40 yearly on account of his three boarders.

The new agent at Rome communicated to the Scotch Bishops the congratulations of Propaganda on the repeal of the penal laws. They thanked and praised the excellent Sovereign of Great Britain, and extolled the Bishop's pastoral letter, as it was designed to express the gratitude of the Scotch Catholics and to encourage them in piety and religion. The Cardinal, however, held out no hopes of a national president for the Scotch College. The agent, although a young man, wisely advised the more prudent policy of not pressing for a change at that time, especially as the discipline of the College happened to be tolerably good. Cardinal Antonelli bore high testimony to the excellent state of the Scotch mission. This was some compensation to the Bishops for the rejection of their plans. "There was no mission," he said, "connected with Propaganda that gave the congregation so much pleasure as the Scotch." Mr. McPherson, it appears, had better success with Albani than with the Cardinal Prefect of Propaganda. He was allowed a certain charge of the students in the Scotch College. This was welcome news to Bishop Hay, who looked upon the concession as providential, and indicative of still better things to come. There was no longer any difficulty about sending boys to Rome. It would now be an easy matter to fill the College if only some provision could be made for travelling expenses.

Mr. Maxwell, of Munshes, to whose efforts the Catholics were, in great measure, indebted for the Relief Bill, did not long survive to enjoy the benefit of his successful exertions. He was thrown from his horse in September, and died unconscious, the third day after the accident. As he was a benefactor of the mission Bishop Hay called on all the clergy to celebrate thrice for the repose of his soul. Having died without making a will, his sister Mrs. Maxwell of Terraughty, inherited all his fortune. Her husband, although a Protestant, permitted Mr. Robertson and two emigrant French priests to remain undisturbed at Munshes.

There died this year, also, to the great regret of many friends, another friend of the mission, Miss Dorothy Riddell, aunt to the Laird of Kirkconnell. This benefactress bequeathed to the mission £1,000.

Monseigneur Erskine on arriving at |Edinburgh, paid a visit to Bishop Hay. He had the interests of the Scotch College at Rome much at heart. He had great influence with Cardinals Albani and Talada as well as the Holy Father himself; and he promised to use it in favour of the mission. He also took into consideration the proposal to induce the British Government to move in the affair of national superiors. He had charge, on occasion of visiting his relations in Great Britain, to testify when opportunity occurred the grateful sense which his masters entertained of the favours lately bestowed on Catholics in Britain and of the deliverance of the Italian States from the dangers which lately threatened them. Monseigneur Erskine was graciously received by some of the higher people in London. He promised on his return from visiting his relations in Fifeshire to pay another visit to Bishop Hay.

It affords pleasure to find that Bishop Geddes, notwithstanding his great sufferings, was still able to apply to literary work. In compliance with the request of the Roman Prelate, Bishop Hay begged of him to dictate to Mr. Gordon a rough sketch of the principal subjects which he thought should be alluded to in the intended account of mission affairs. Bishop Geddes remarked that nothing would occur to him that his friend would not also think of. His idea was that the account of mission affairs should be drawn up in the form of a letter to the Prelate, beginning with an appropriate acknowledgment of their confidence in him. They might assure him and beg him to assure others, that none could be more sincerely attached to the Holy See than they were, both from a sense of duty and also out of the warmest gratitude for its paternal care. They might add their resolution always to instil similar sentiments into the people under their charge; and always to live so as to do honour to religion and to prove themselves not unworthy of the favour and protection of the established Government. It might also be said that the only exception to the perfect unanimity of the Catholic clergy was the unhappy dispute with Principal Gordon, of which it might be well to give Mgr. Erskine a short outline. The report might, likewise, allude to the fact that public prejudice against them had greatly subsided, and that an ample field of usefulness had been thrown open to them by the late Act of Parliament, but one which they must occupy with great caution and prudence, in the face of latent bigotry without, and of a latitudinarian spirit within their own body. They might then proceed to inform Mgr. Erskine of the number, the position and the circumstances of the Catholic body. Their number might be stated at 25,000 ; but of that Bishop Hay was the best judge. They might mention the emigrants to America and the departure of three or four missionaries to Canada. The report might lay before the Roman Prelate a statement of the resources on which the clergy depended for their maintenance ; which, although lately augmented by a few legacies, had, on the whole, been considerably diminished by the French Revolution. An attempt had been made to induce their people to contribute something towards the support of the clergy, and not altogether in vain. But in some parts of the country living was dear, and their people very poor. The number of missionaries, already too small for the demands made on their services, was likely to be further diminished by the recent loss of their French seminaries at Paris and Douai; although it was to be hoped that this loss would only be temporary. At that time the whole dependence of the mission rested on the Scotch Colleges at Rome and Valladolid. An application made by the Roman Prelate to the Spanish Ministry might be of service to the Seminary at Valladolid; and his interference on behalf of the Roman College would confer on the mission a still more signal benefit. He might be made to understand that the Scotch Bishops desired above everything to see that College placed under the charge of Scotch Superiors, who would naturally know best what was best to be taught in preparation for a missionary life in Scotland, and would most naturally take a deeper interest than foreigners could in the success of the College. The Bishops could not desire a better Superior for it than their present agent in Rome. It was much to be wished, also, that Mgr. Erskine could obtain for the College the means of supporting twelve students. His attention, moreover, should be called to the inefficient state of the Scotch Monasteries in Germany, with a view to his concurring with the Bishops in their endeavours to effect an alteration in their Constitutions if the Monks could be brought to acquiesce. Lastly,

CATHOLICS OF SCOTLAND. 611

the subject would be exhausted if a significant hint accompanied the description of the home seminaries and their present state, that, in the preceding century, Propaganda had, for some years, maintained two schoolmasters in the Highlands.

On occasion of sending the above suggestions to Bishop Hay, Bishop Geddes requested that the Bishop would send to Dr. Gleig, a copy of "The Papist Misrepresented and Represented." He stated, also, that his health was pretty much the same; only that he was getting more accustomed to his weakness and felt it less in consequence. As it was the last day of the year he concluded by wishing his friends many happy returns.

The missionaries and principal Catholics of Scotland had by this time pretty generally taken the Oath of Allegiance; and it was announced in the newspapers that they had done so. Notwithstanding the late partial repeal of the penal laws, the spirit of intolerance was far from being laid; and in several parts of the country attempts were still made to curtail the measure of liberty permitted by the law. The Catholics, therefore, in a body, applied to the law officers of the Crown in Scotland for information as to the precise limits of their liberty on certain disputed points. (January 16, 1794.) Three of these related to the celebration of mar : 1st.—Was it necessary for them to proclaim their banns of marriage in the Parish Church, or would not proclamation in their own chapel suffice? 2nd.—Must they be married by the Minister of the parish or submit to a fine? 3rd.—And if one of the parties were a Protestant, and was willing to be married by the Priest, was that Protestant party exposed to Church censures and a fine? The Lord Advocate and the Solicitor-General, in a joint paper, informed the Memorialists that the law on these points had not been changed. It was still necessary that banns of marriage should be proclaimed in the Parish Church; and no one but a minister of the establishment was permitted to celebrate a marriage with the sole exception, made in the reign of Queen Ann, in favour of the Episcopal Clergy. An infringement of these conditions still rendered the parties liable to all the serious penalties attached to clandestine marriages. To a query relating to the registration of Catholic infants in the books of the parish, it was answered that no obligation lay on any one whether Catholic or Protestant, to register his child in the parish books; but the utility of the practice ought to recommend it to every one. Was it imperative on a Catholic who had given public scandal to submit to public censures in the established Church? The Memorialists were informed that a refusal to submit to such a censure involved no civil penalties, entailing nothing more than excommunication or exclusion from the spiritual privileges of the establishment, a penalty which plainly could have no force in the case of persons who were already separated from that communion. No law existed to prevent a Catholic Priest from baptising any child if the parents desired it, even the illegitimate children of Protestant parents regarding whom the inquiry had been made. Nevertheless in parishes where the session clerk and the beadle had uniformly and immemorially claimed their dues for Baptism, Catholics, like all other persons residing in those parishes, were legally bound to pay them even in the case where neither session clerk nor beadle were asked to officiate.

CAP. L.

FURTHER INQUIRY AS TO THE STATE OF THE LAW—THE CATHOLICS LOYAL SUBJECTS---STATESMEN FRIENDLY ---MGR. ERSKINE AT EDINBURGH--AT LONDON--CORRESPONDS WITH BISHOP GEDDES—HIS ADMIRATION OF EDINBURGH—BISHOP GEDDES, ALTHOUGH ILL, ENGAGED IN WRITING A LIFE OF SAINT MARGARET—WRITES ALSO ON THE SCOTCH MISSION, AND FOR ENCYCLOPEDIA BRITANNICA---DR. GLEIG, THE EDITOR MUCH PLEASED—THE DECLINE OF TRADE AT GLASGOW SERIOUSLY AFFECTS THE HIGHLANDERS—SOME HIGHLAND GENTLEMEN MEET AT FORT AUGUSTUS—RESOLVE TO RAISE A CATHOLIC REGIMENT—THEIR OFFER AT FIRST DECLINED—FINALLY ACCEPTED—BISHOP HAY PERSUADED TO FORWARD THE SCHEME—CAUSES OF OPPOSITION—THE REGIMENT IN IRELAND—SHAMEFUL CONDUCT OF THE YEOMANRY—IN 1802, THE REGIMENT DISBANDED—THE CHAPLAIN OBTAINS LAND FOR THE DISBANDED MEN IN CANADA—THE HIGHLANDERS HIGHLY PRAISED—THE ONLY PEOPLE FROM WHOM NO COMPLAINT WAS EVER HEARD—MR. MCDONELL'S DISINTERESTEDNESS—RECOMMENDS AN ORGANIZED MILITARY EMIGRATION TO BRITISH NORTH AMERICA.

Did the law, the Memorialists further inquired, authorize masters in schools supported by the Society for the Propagation of Christian knowledge, to force Catholic children to learn the Protestant catechism, or to expel them in case of refusal? The practice, it was added, was a pernicious one to the children, as their minds became confused between the lessons of the school-master and their parents' instructions at home. In reply it was stated that the practice of schools supported by the society in question was regulated solely by its private rules. Any complaints, therefore, that the Memorialists might have to make must be addressed to the managers of the society who alone had it in their power to grant or refuse any request made to them.

"Are not the Catholics, by the late Act in their favour, put on an equal footing, at least as to all the above articles, with His Majesty's other subjects who are of a different communion from the established Church?" Such was the final query of the Memorialists. They must have derived but little comfort from the answer of the lawyers. "Having given specific answers to all the above queries, an answer to this one appears almost unnecessary. The purpose of the late Act of Parliament is clearly expressed, both in the preamble and the enactment, to have been merely this, to enable Roman Catholics to hold and enjoy property of all kinds without molestation on account of their religious persuasion, and to substitute in place of the formula (by which they were obliged under the Act of King William to renounce their religion) an oath of abjuration and declaration sufficient to secure their allegiance to the King and to the Constitution of the country." If words mean anything, these words amounted to this : we are unwilling to remind you that so far from being on an equal footing with your fellow-subjects, all that the late Act did for you was to enable you to possess your own property without absolutely denying your religion. The memorial of the Catholics concluded in these words: "The Roman Catholics beg leave to observe that they propose the above queries by no means with any view or wish to be exempted from what the laws of their country required, but only to know what these laws require from them that they may faithfully observe them and not be exposed to illegal severities and impositions with which people of unfriendly dispositions may endeavour to distress them. They are and wish to give every proof in their power of their being faithful subjects, good citizens and worthy members of society, and they humbly apprehend that the late indulgence granted them by the Legislature entitles them to be treated as such while they behave themselves conformably to these characters, especially in matters where their consciences are interested and in which they wish to give offence to no man. They beg leave further to observe that they do not want to be exempted from such legal Kirk dues as are required in any of the above cases and are paid by other non-conformists; but as they observe that such dues are never exacted from other non-conformists and rigourously demanded from Catholics, and when exacted, are sometimes more, sometimes less, at the arbitrium of the Kirk session; they, therefore, wish to know what the law precisely requires on this head, that they may not be exposed to the arbitrary imposition of people prejudiced against them." So, as the learned lawyers pointed out, there remained some unpleasant disabilities to await the action of a more enlightened age. No doubt, the statesmen of the day did their best, and succeeded in removing the more unjust and harassing points of the penal code; but they judged, and perhaps wisely, that something must be left to satisfy the cravings of blind bigotry. Of the remaining evils there was none that inflicted any serious hardship; but they were exceedingly galling, vexatious and humiliating. What, for instance, could be more so than the legal obligation Catholics still lay under to have their marriage banns proclaimed in the "parish church," as the Presbyterian meeting house was called? What purpose could it serve to make this proclamation in the midst of a congregation of strangers to the parties proclaimed? If there were any valid objection to the union of such parties it must be best known in the congregation to which they belonged.

There appears to have been a want of courtesy on the part of Mgr. Erskine when at Edinburgh, returning from the North. He spent ten days in the city without ever returning any one of Bishop Hay's frequent visits to him. This was disappointing, as the Bishop hoped by a personal interview to obtain something in favour of the Scotch College at Rome. On his return to London he was received at Court on the King's Birthday. This favourable reception he owed, no doubt, to his connection with a noble family as well as to the friendly relations of Great Britain with Rome. It is noteworthy that even the newspapers alluded without disapprobation to the fact that he was a secret envoy from the Court of Rome. In the month of May he wrote to Bishop Geddes, in reply to two letters which the Bishop had addressed to him when he was in Scotland. It gave him the greatest pleasure, he said, to learn how much the Bishop was esteemed and loved by his numerous acquaintance in Scotland. He had been as far north as St. Andrews and found the climate very mild, although it was winter. Notwithstanding that he was born in a distant country, he experienced on approaching Cambo, his family seat, sensations such as arise on revisiting after a long absence, one's paternal home. His mention of Edinburgh is particularly complimentary to that city. "It was a charming town. Every view of it and from it is picturesque; and that mixture of old and of new, engages not only the eye, but also the imagination. As for its society, I must say it is the pleasantest I ever met with; and I shall never forget the civilities I received there." He had been lately appointed auditor to the Pope, a dignity next to that of Cardinal, and a near step to the Cardinalate. His predecessor, Cardinal Roverella, was to continue to act for him till his return to Rome.

There was great sympathy, meanwhile, with the invalid Bishop amongst his many friends. Among the rest, Lord Monboddo frequently inquired for him of the clergy at Edinburgh. If he were not fully restored to health it would not be for the want of the good wishes of all classes at the capital, and he would not have to remain long at Aberdeen. It afforded him great comfort in the trying times of illness, that he was able to apply to literary composition. He engaged in preparing a life of Saint Margaret, founding on the biography written in Italian by Father Aloysius Leslie. Other literary projects, moreover, occupied his mind. He had begun to dictate a series of reflections on the affairs of the Scotch mission, and had finished a preliminary chapter on the choice of boys for the seminaries. He also proposed writing an account of the state of religion in Scotland during the troubled years of 1745 and 1746. In addition to all this the Bishop was able to write articles for the *Encyclopedia Britannica*. He had finished one on the subject of the Pope, with which the editor, Dr. Gleig, was much pleased. It was to be published in a few weeks. The Bishop had another paper in preparation. The subject was his former Professor, Boscovich and his Theory of Corpuscular Attraction. This was very gratifying to Professor Robison of the University of Edinburgh. Dr. Gleig declared that he had seldom seen a man to whom any news gave more delight than to the Professor when he was told that Bishop Geddes had undertaken to write a life of Boscovich. Professor Robison was a great admirer of the Italian philosopher, considering him scarcely inferior to Newton himself. His own views on Boscovich had not been published. Some of these he promised to impart to the Bishop.

The disturbed state of the European continent affected so seriously the manufacturing trade of Glasgow, that the Highlanders, who had faithfully served the manufacturers during two years, lost their employment. This unfortunate state of matters induced some gentlemen connected with the Highlands, to hold a meeting at Fort Augustus, in order to consult as to the best means of providing for the people who had been thrown out of employment. At this meeting it was resolved that they should offer to raise a regiment consisting entirely of Catholics under a Colonel who should also be a Catholic and having a Catholic priest for chaplain. This was, no doubt, a bold measure, especially as a similar offer had been made some years before and declined. Bishop Hay, when asked to give his assistance, could not at first consent. He had many misgivings, and would not allow Rev. Alex. McDonell to leave his charge at Glasgow even temporarily to attend the meeting at Fort Augustus. The Bishop went himself to Glasgow, and after conferring with the proposed chaplain and the youthful chief, Glengarry, who was to have the command of the intended regiment, having also seen letters from Bishop Chisholm and other Highland gentlemen, entered warmly into the scheme, had the report of the meeting copied for distribution amongst the Lowland gentry and introduced a deputation from the Fort Augustus meeting to the Lord Advocate. The Bishop appears to have been favourably impressed with the candour and politeness of the parties whom he met at Glasgow. He was "much edified," he said, with Glengarry. "He is an amiable young gentleman, and I hope will one day be an honour and support to his country and to religion." In London the deputation met with great civility. They found there the Lord Advocate and his uncle, Henry Dundas, the Home Secretary, who presented the address of the meeting to His Majesty the King. In a few days the Secretary of State informed them that His Majesty viewed with much approbation so great a proof of the loyalty of His Majesty's subjects in Scotland, but, that, in existing circumstances, he felt it to be necessary to decline their offer of a regiment. The Rev. A. McDonell was now ill, for some time, in consequence of disappointment and over exertion. Notwithstanding, he and his chief persevered in their application. They obtained another interview with Mr. Dundas, who listened favourably to the exposition of their views as to the effects of the Highland emigration. In ten days they were again invited to an interview, at which Mr. Dundas received them with much politeness, and, after some further discussion, gave them hopes of obtaining the command of a fencible regiment for the young Highland chief. Opposition was made, meanwhile, by the fascinating Duchess of

Gordon, whose son, the Marquess of Huntly, was at the time raising a regiment, and the majority of his dependants being Catholics would, no doubt, have preferred to enlist in a Catholic regiment. Another Highland chief, Sir James Grant, for a like cause, opposed the scheme. Notwithstanding all opposition, however, Glengarry finally obtained his regiment. It was recruited largely from the Highlands; and Mr. McDonell was appointed its chaplain, although for his appointment it was necessary to evade the existing law. It was no slight recommendation to the regiment that it volunteered to serve in any part of Great Britain or Ireland, Jersey or Guernsey, several other Scotch volunteer regiments having refused to serve even in England. This offer was very acceptable to the Government, as it established a precedent for all fencible corps that might afterwards be raised. The first service of the new regiment was in the Isle of Guernsey which, in 1795, was threatened with invasion by the French. It remained there till the breaking out of the Irish rebellion in 1798. It was in that year ordered to Ireland. The most disturbed parts of the country were destined to be the scene of their services, the Government relying on the good conduct, bravery and activity of the mountaineer soldiers. The counties of Wicklow and Wexford, together with the mountainous regions and swamps of Connemara, where the most lawless characters had taken refuge, and who frequently issued from their fastnesses during the night to harass the peaceably disposed inhabitants and burn their houses and outbuildings, presented a wide field to the prowess and good management of the Glengarry regiment. Mr. McDonell, acting in the twofold capacity of chaplain to the regiment and counsel to the chief, was able to prevent the excesses so generally indulged in, and by which the native yeomanry, especially, won for themselves unenviable distinction, and became objects of terror and detestation to the insurgent inhabitants. There was no kind of outrage of which they were not guilty. They seized the Catholic churches in the counties of Wicklow, Carlow and Wexford, and made stables of them for their horses. At first the Highlanders also inspired terror. If their own fellow-countrymen acted so cruelly and so profanely, what might the people not expect of those semi-nude barbarians from the mountains of Scotland? They were speedily undeceived. The chief, acting in concert with the chaplain, restored the churches to their proper uses and invited the clergy and congregations to resume possession. They caused the soldiers to clean them and adapt them once more for the purposes of religious worship. The Highlanders, indeed, like the yeomanry hunted in the least accessible places, but for a very different purpose. They searched for and found the hunted down and terrified inhabitants, and brought them back to their devastated fields and deserted homes. This was not the usual way of quelling rebellions. It was, however, an effectual one, and worthy of an enlightened age. Peace and order were soon restored throughout all the districts assigned to the Highland soldiers. The people everywhere returned with joy to their churches and dwellings, relying on the protection of parties who had no interest to deceive them.

At the peace of 1802 the Glengarry regiment was disbanded, and its members were again reduced to great difficulty, the Scotch manufacturing trade having been so circumscribed by the late sanguinary war that the Highlanders could not find an asylum or employment in their own country. In these circumstances Mr. McDonell began to entertain the hope that he might establish for them a claim upon the Government, in so far as to obtain for them grants of land in Upper Canada, where so many of their friends were already settled on lands given as rewards for services rendered during the American Revolutionary War. In furtherance of this view the Rev. Alexander McDonell repaired to London, and sought an interview with Premier Addington. The

Minister received him with the greatest cordiality, complimented him on the bravery and loyalty of his countrymen, and assured him that nothing would give him greater pleasure than to afford substantial proof of the good will of His Majesty's Government towards them, inasmuch as, of all His Majesy's subjects, the Highlanders were always the readiest to come forward at their country's call, and the only class from whom a complaint had never been heard. Mr. Addington further declared to Mr. McDonell that nothing gave him deeper cause of regret than to see such brave and loyal subjects forced by adverse circumstances to the necessity of quitting their native land to seek in a distant country subsistence for themselves and families. The Minister desired to induce Mr. McDonell to take his people to the Island of Trinidad, which, shortly before, had been ceded by Spain to Great Britain. Mr. McDonell was offered there, for every head of a family, eighty acres of land, as much money as would suffice to place four slaves on every farm, a physician and a schoolmaster for the new colony, and for a period of three years as much wine for the use of the colonists as he and the doctor should consider necessary for the preservation of their health. He himself, moreover, and some special professional friends, whose services, no doubt, would be required, were promised such salaries as would make them independent. These were tempting inducements. Mr. McDonell, nevertheless, felt that it was for him a sacred duty to decline the Minister's well-meant propositions. He had, hitherto, he said, in reply to Mr. Addington, devoted his life to the good of his fellow-creatures. He could not now think of persuading them to emigrate to an unhealthy tropical climate. Having declined the magnificent offer of the Premier, Mr. McDonell renewed his solicitation for a grant of land in Upper Canada. Mr. Addington at first objected to granting Mr. McDonell's request, on the ground that the hold of the British Government on the Province of Upper Canada was so slight that he did not think himself warranted in encouraging the King's loyal subjects to emigrate to that colony. Mr. McDonell, on the other hand, assured the Minister that the emigration of the Highlanders to Upper Canada would form the strongest possible tie between that colony and the parent state. He, moreover, suggested at the same time, the advantage that would accrue to Great Britain by organizing the disbanded Fencibles into a military emigration to the British Provinces of North America and granting to them land after a limited period of service. If such a measure had been adopted much trouble that afterwards arose would probably have been averted.

CAP. LI.

THE HIGHLAND LANDLORDS OPPOSE EMIGRATION—MR. M'DONELL, NOTWITHSTANDING ALL DIFFICULTIES, BRINGS HIS PEOPLE TO CANADA IN THE YEAR 1803-4—APPOINTED TO ST. RAPHAEL'S—HOW HE LANDED—INCIDENT AT KINGSTON—OBTAINING PATENTS FOR EARLIER SETTLERS; AND THEN FOR HIS OWN—THE MOSES OF HIS PEOPLE—PROVIDES CHURCHES—PAPAL ENVOYS—THE PRESS FAVOURS THEM—NARRATIVE OF REPEAL IN ITALIAN—THE POPE THANKED FOR OPENING HIS PORTS TO THE BRITISH FLEET AND ENTERTAINING BRITISH TROOPS—A GOLD MEDAL TO EVERY OFFICER—MR. HIPPISLEY—STUDENTS—BISHOP HAY IN LONDON—EMIGRANT FRENCH CLERGY ON DUTY IN SCOTLAND—CASE OF A FRENCH PRIEST—BISHOP GEDDES ABLE TO APPLY TO LITERARY PURSUITS—BISHOP HAY ON SOME OF THE CLERGY—MR. CHARLES GORDON—BISHOP GEDDES' DIFFICULTIES.

At length, in March, 1803, Mr. McDonell obtained the sign manual for a grant of land to every officer and soldier of the Glengarry regiment whom he should introduce into Upper Canada. Such good fortune must meet with opposition. As soon as the fact became known the Highland proprietors took alarm and endeavoured by every means that could be thought of to prevent their people from emigrating. The regulations of the Emigrant Act were rigidly enforced, and many of the poor men, after selling their effects and repairing with their families to the ports of embarkation, were not permitted to leave the country. Such was the effect produced by the fears and threats of the Highland lairds on the Home Ministry, that even Lord Hobart, Colonial Secretary of State, urged Mr. McDonell to conduct his emigrants to Upper Canada, by way of the United States, in order that the odium of directly assisting emigration from the Highlands might be avoided, there being at that time a Provincial Law which granted 200 acres of land to every loyal subject entering Upper Canada from the United States with the intention to settle in the Province. Mr. McDonell could not be guided by this advice; and, heedless of opposition, made his way to Upper Canada with his followers, as he best could, in the years 1803-4. He may be said to have actually smuggled away his people, so numerous and so vexatious were the restrictions that stood in the way of their departure.

Mr. McDonell landed in Quebec in 1803, and was immediately appointed to the mission of St. Raphael, Upper Canada. A remarkable incident occurred at his landing. There were no wharves in those days at Quebec. What happened in consequence may well be alluded to as showing the extraordinarily powerful physique which characterized the Highlanders of a generation or two ago. The ship lay out in the river, and Mr. McDonell was considering the best way of getting ashore, when, as he himself related to Chevalier W. J. MacDonell, of Toronto, " a fine strapping young fellow waded out to the ship, took me in his arms as if I had been a baby, and carried me ashore." This "fine strapping young fellow" was the Chevalier's uncle, John McDonell, in his day a renowned "North Wester," who died about forty years ago, at his residence, Point Fortune, on the Ottawa. It has been well remarked: "there were giants in those days." Mr. McDonell, the chaplain, was himself a man of herculean stature, six feet four inches in height and stout in proportion. What, then, must not the fine fellow who carried him so easily have been? Bishop McDonell related, as the Chevalier informs us, that Colonel John McDonell, the father of the young fellow, John McDonell, one Spring morning, when the ice was breaking up, ran into his son's room and cried out, "John, you are a pretty fellow to be lying abed at this time of day, while a poor man is being carried down the river on a cake of ice." John at once leapt from his couch, hastened down to the river, plunged in, "*un*accoutred as he was," rescued the man who was on the point of perishing, and returned in triumph to the paternal dwelling.

The ex-chaplain's strength and courage were not inferior to his stature. Later, when Bishop at Kingston, which was at that time a hot bed of Orangeism, he was called upon, together with his Vicar-General, Mr. William McDonald, one 12th of July, to assist in quelling a riot. His splendid figure was conspicuous. A worthy disciple of King William (*unworthy* we should say, for King William opposed all he could the enacting of the penal laws), in a state of great excitement, pressed through the crowd, declaring his intention to have "a hit at that big antiChrist." The Bishop looked at him, and in his calm, deliberate manner, *jerked out:* "It would be the dearest blow that ever you struck." The *pretended disciple* instantly subsided.

On arriving in Upper Canada, Mr. McDonell presented his credentials to Lieutenant-General Hunter, who was at the time Lieutenant-Governor of the Province, and obtained for his followers the land allotted to them according to the Sign Manual. He took up his residence in the County of Glengarry, and had there his chief dwelling place for a quarter of a century. Very few of the emigrants who had previously arrived in the country had procured legal tenures for the lands on which they were settled. In consequence of this state of matters, he repaired to York, and, after a good deal of trouble, obtained patent deeds for 160,000 acres of land in favour of his new clients. After some further delay, patents for the lands of his own followers were also secured. Thus, Mr. McDonell, the Moses of his people, if he did not conduct them through a wilderness, brought them in safety over the great ocean, notwithstanding the most formidable opposition, and established them, although not in a land actually flowing with milk and honey, in a country that abounds in every product conducive to healthful life. His next care was to provide churches, of which there were only three in the whole Province on his arrival, two of wood and one a stone building. There were no more than two priests, one a Frenchman who knew not a word of the English language, the other an Irishman who soon afterwards left the country. There was, thus, a vast field for Mr. McDonell's missionary labours ; and he devoted himself to them during the remainder of his days.

Having seen our Catholic Highlanders, under the guidance of Mr. McDonell, securely and permanently settled in Canada, we go back a few years and find an English gentleman, Sir John Hippisley, who was a member of Parliament and a Protestant, laudably endeavouring to establish diplomatic relations between the Courts of Rome and Great Britain. It was no secret that Papal envoys, although not publicly recognized as such, had been already received at the British Court. Such was Mgr. Erskine; and Sir John Hippisley had been similarly employed. The newspapers of the day, in alluding to these well-known facts, expressed no disapprobation. It was in contemplation, even to introduce into Parliament a measure for establishing official relations between the British and Roman Courts. In order to prepare the way for so great a change, Mr. Hippisley had charge to ask the Scotch agent at Rome, in the name of his Government, to supply any documents proving the desire of Propaganda that the British Catholics should live in submission to the established Government, especially in the years 1715 and 1745. It was of great importance to secure the favour of the Pope to the proposed measure. Mr. Hippisley, accordingly, asked for an Italian translation of a narrative of the repeal of the penal laws in England which Mr. Macpherson had given to Cardinal Antonelli. This translation, Mr. Hippisley delivered with his own hand to the Holy Father. Although not at Rome in the quality of an ambassador, Mr. Hippisley possessed more influence than all the foreign ambassadors together. The envoy from England was in high favour with the British Catholics at Rome. The clergy, secular and regular, joined in a public address to him, testifying their appreciation of his strenuous endeavours to establish anew friendly relations between the British and Roman Courts, whilst at the same time showing much friendliness to Catholics generally. The British Catholics resident at Rome, in like manner, expressed the gratification afforded them by the conduct of the Pope in opening his ports for the supply of the British fleet, and by causing a British regiment of cavalry to be honourably received and entertained for three months in the Papal States. The Pope, moreover, as a mark of his special esteem for the British nation, presented each officer with a gold medal. The negotiations conducted by Mr. Hippisley, no doubt, largely contributed towards these friendly intercommunications. This was expressed in the address, which also alluded to the approbation by the British Cabinet of Mr. Hippisley's diplomatic services and the esteem which they had won for him among all the members of the Roman Court. Parties who took a deep interest in these matters, now hoped to see the diplomatist speedily appointed British Minister at the Papal Court. It was suggested that the Bishops of Scotland should present to Mr. Hippisley, a complimentary address. Mgr. Erskine, however, advised that a private assurance of their gratitude for his services would be more to the purpose in the actual state of matters. Bishop Geddes, accordingly, addressed to Mr. Hippisley a polite private letter. In reply, the diplomatist assured him of his own friendly dispositions and those of the British Government towards the Holy See and the Catholics of Great Britain, in whose behalf he hoped to see substantial justice finally meted out by the nation.

Some students from Douai, who were destined for Valladolid, may be mentioned here, as their names were long familiar to many Catholics of more recent times. They were William Wallace, so long chaplain, afterwards, at Traquair; Alexander Badenoch, known, for several years, as an able and edifying priest at Edinburgh, and George Gordon, for a long time highly esteemed in the North, as the priest of Dufftown. In their voyage from London to Spain, they were driven, by stress of weather, as far as the coast of Brazil. They were three months on their passage; and it cost the mission £100, in addition to the expense of their journey from Oporto to Valladolid. The Principal there did not think that the talents of Mr. Wallace were equal to those of his two companions. But he described him as solid, very exact in the performance of his duties, and, withal, a friend of his books. This was a moderate estimate. If Mr. Wallace had applied his abilities to general literature he would have figured among the lights of his time. Some controversial writings which only he produced, like most works of the kind, are now forgotten. The Principal gave Mr. Badenoch credit for talents as well as uncommon application; and, what was even of more importance, he possessed the art of securing the affection of his companions and the confidence of his superiors. Mr. Gordon he spoke of as a boy of talents who would advance in learning. (Letter of Principal Gordon to Bishop Geddes.)

About this time Bishop Hay, after visiting his invalid coadjutor at Aberdeen, repaired to London, where he was hospitably entertained at the house of Bishop Douglas. He paid a visit to Mr. Burke, who had so ably advocated in Parliament the cause of the Catholics. This celebrated statesman, together with Mrs. Burke, received the Scotch Bishop with the utmost cordiality; and the visit was repeated the following week. He also visited Monsignor Colbert, Bishop of Rhodez, who had done signal service in the dispute with Principal Gordon. This excellent Prelate introduced him to the emigrant Bishop, St. Pol de Leon. At their interview was discussed the subject of employing some of the French emigrant priests on the Scotch mission. Several of them were already labouring with much acceptance in Bishop Gibson's district. There was a second interview on the subject; but Bishop Hay would come to no determination without consulting his coadjutor. There had been no falling off in Mgr. Erskine's friendship. The Bishop dined at that Prelate's house in company with Bishops Gibson and Douglas. On his return to Scotland Bishop Hay considered anew the question of employing some of the emigrant clergy. Shortly before his visit to London two of them were engaged in teaching French and drawing in the University of St. Andrews. From what he had heard and seen of the emigrants in London he was much inclined to have some of them on the mission. He had a long conversation with one of them whom Mgr. St. Pol de Leon had introduced to him. The Bishop represented to the young priest the difficulties and hardships both as regarded food and labour that must be encountered in the mission. It came to his knowledge afterwards that the young emigrant had been hurt by his observations, as they seemed to imply a suspicion that the difficulties referred to would discourage him. All that those unfortunate exiles desired was that they should be independent of public support. In return for their services they asked only food and clothing. Many of them were applying diligently to the study of the English language. Bishop Hay met with some whose proficiency was very great. The opinion of his coadjutor appears to have been in harmony with his own; for, before the end of the year, there were six emigrant French priests on duty in Scotland. From their anxiety to make for themselves an independent livelihood, many of the emigrants sought to subsist by teaching in parts of the country where there were no Catholics. One of these applied to Bishop Hay for permission to say Mass without a server and without any person being present. This good priest, who was formerly Vicar-General of Lisieux, taught French in a part of the country where it was impossible to hear Mass, and where there was not a single Catholic. Considering the circumstances, the Bishop gave him permission, according to his application, on Sundays and holidays. But afterwards, doubting his authority in the matter, he applied specially to the Holy See.

Bishop Geddes, meanwhile, although the weakness in his arms and hands was increasing, continued to apply with his usual diligence to literary pursuits, and completed this summer his paper on Catholic affairs in Scotland in the years 1745-46.

He contemplated writing a life of Boscovich and was expecting from Rome some materials for the purpose. The agent there informed him that a fellow-countyman of his was collecting matter for a biography of the admirable Creighton. Perhaps the Bishop could throw some light on his history? To this the invalid replied that the life written by Sir Thomas Urquhart, which he had read long ago, was of suspicious authority; and some of the statements were proved absolutely false by their anachronisms. The late Lord Hailes had published a life of Creighton. There was also an account of him in the *British Biography*. But the most authentic history of him that Bishop Geddes had ever seen, was inserted in the dedication of Cicero's *Paradoxa* (inscribed to Creighton by Aldus Minutius the younger,) and in the annotations of that work. It was published about the year 1581, when Creighton was actually at Venice.

The small chapel house at Aberdeen, in which the invalid Bishop resided, was now well filled. Beside the Bishop's nephew, Mr. John Gordon, who was the officiating priest of Aberdeen, there were Mr. Farquarson and three Douai students who had been lately boarding in Glenlivat with Mr. Paterson. These four occupied the upper story. This last arrangement had not proved satisfactory, owing chiefly to the impracticable character of Mr. Andrew Carruthers, who, when Bishop Hay remonstrated with him, wrote a long reply "taking to pieces" all that the Bishop had said.—(Bishop Hay to Bishop Geddes, Jan. 10th). This little seminary was shortly joined by Mr. Andrew Scott, who had passed the preceding winter with Bishop Hay at Edinburgh. Mr. Farquarson's office was that of preparing the four youths for ordination. One of them soon abandoned his studies. Another was Mr. Charles Gordon, so long known afterwards as the worthy priest of Aberdeen. Mr. Farquarson, in communicating these facts to the agent at Rome, informed him, at the same time, that his worthy and afflicted friend, Bishop Geddes, suffered much at times, and that he signed his name with difficulty. It would melt a tiger's heart, he added, to see the best of men thus exhausted before his time. His days are full, though less numerous than might have been expected. He retained, however, Mr. Farquarson thought, his mental faculties better than ever. In addition to his bodily affliction three or four years of his Spanish pension remained unpaid, and he was involved in church affairs. His allowance from Rome was inconsiderable; and hence he was in straitened circumstances.

CAP. LII.

A STRANGE SALE—BAD PRINCIPLES SPREADING—THE CASE OF DOWNIE—COLLEGE IN ENGLAND—ENGLISH "CATHOLIC COMMITTEE" AND "CIS ALPINE-CLUB" SUBMIT TO THE BISHOPS—BISHOP HAY AND MR. BURKE—MGR. ERSKINE, THE PAPAL ENVOY, VERY FRIENDLY—STUDENTS UNABLE TO GO ABROAD—TAUGHT BY BISHOP CHISHOLM---VISITORS AT SCALAN—BISHOPS MEET AT GIBSTON—BISHOP HAY CONTINUED IN PROCURATORSHIP—LETTERS TO ROME—NUMBER OF CATHOLICS 45,000—AN AMERICAN PRIEST IN OFFICE AT THE SCOTCH COLLEGE, ROME.—TWO PLACES IN PROPAGANDA COLLEGE TO SCOTCH STUDENTS—MR. FARQUARSON SUCCEEDS MR. M'DONELL AT GLASGOW—THE FAMILIES OF GUELPH AND STEWART RECONCILED—LITERARY LABOURS OF BISHOP GEDDES— HIS DIFFICULTIES—GREATER EDUCATION FACILITIES NECESSARY—THE DUKE OF GORDON LIBERAL TOWARDS CATHOLICS—PRAYERS FOR THE KING.

It pained the suffering Bishop moreover, to learn on inquiring of his friend, the agent, that the portrait of Baron Menzies of Pitfodels, which was in the recreation room of the Scotch College, together with other portraits, all the English books and most of the classics in every language, had been sold by the late rector, in the Piazza Navona. No wonder if the Bishops made every exertion to have a national President appointed.

As a warning to all Catholics in times of political agitation, the case of one Downie, a member of the Edinburgh congregation, comes now to be recorded. The principles of the French Revolution were spreading over all the countries of Europe. Scotland was not exempt from the contagion. At Edinburgh there was formed an association which called itself "Friends of the People." It was believed to be in correspondence with the French convention, perhaps even subsidized by it. This society, in the course of the year, fell into the hands of justice. The ring-leaders, and among the rest the Unitarian minister of Dundee, were tried and transported. This warning was lost upon the association. It still persisted in its treasonable designs. A second disclosure was made when pike heads of a deadly shape were discovered. These weapons combined the properties of a pike, an axe and a small scythe. Watt, a wine merchant, in whose house they were first found, was arrested, together with a blacksmith named Orrock, who had made them. At first these parties refused to give any information concerning their employers and associates. A few days of more strict imprisonment, however, induced them to speak. It came to light that the pikes had been ordered and paid for by David Downie, a goldsmith, who, for many months, had been associated with the "Friends of the People." This unfortunate man was a member of the small Catholic congregation. He bore a good character and had been advanced to the post of treasurer of the Goldsmiths' Company. He could not claim to be excused for his treasonable practices on the ground of youth, for he was more than sixty years of age. Some time before this man was arrested, Bishop Hay had denounced the "Friends of the People" from the pulpit, insisting, at the same time, on the duties of loyalty and obedience. This denunciation excited Downie's radical enthusiasm, and he said: "The Bishop has turned recruiting sergeant to King George, and I will have nothing more to do with him." He, in pursuance of his threat, gave up attending at the Bishop's chapel.

Watt and Downie were tried for their lives and sentenced to death. Downie now came to a better state of mind, and wrote a penitent letter to Bishop Hay, praying forgiveness and begging of the Bishop to send a priest to prepare him for death. Mr. Alexander Cameron, who succeeded his uncle, Bishop

Geddes, in the rectorship of Valladolid, was appointed for this service. There being some extenuating circumstances in Downie's case, the jury had recommended him to mercy, and a memorial in his behalf was sent to London. Bishop Hay visited him, meanwhile, and did all in his power to console Mrs. Downie and her family. The name of the condemned man was recommended in St. Margaret's chapel to the prayers of the people on the Sunday immediately preceding the day fixed for his execution. He was, however, respited at first for a month; and, afterwards, his sentence was commuted to transportation.

The Bishop was now preparing for the annual meeting at Gibston. From Scalan he wrote to the agent at Rome informing him of the success of his visit to London. He had satisfactorily settled with Bishop Douglas regarding the erection of a College in England, in order to supply the loss of the College at Douai.

It gave him much pleasure to state that the English gentlemen who had taken part in the "Catholic Committee" and afterwards in the "cis Alpine-club," which succeeded it, had given up their mistaken ideas and declared entirely for the Bishops. He mentions his most friendly relations with Mr. Burke, and adds that this illustrious statesman was much pleased to hear of the intention to have a College in England,

and recommended that they should apply to Government for a charter or letters patent in order to render it permanent, giving them to understand, at the same time, that such favour would not be refused. The Bishops standing well at Court would meet with every encouragement. There was no lessening of the Bishop's friendship with the Papal envoy, Mgr. Erskine, who showed him every attention, and shortly before he left the city invited him, together with the English Bishops, and some other gentlemen, to dine with him. The afternoon was spent with the utmost cordiality, to the Bishop's great satisfaction. The wars of the French, but too successful, rendered it dangerous to send students abroad. Bishop Chisholm, in the meantime, directed their studies, so that as little harm as possible should be caused by the delay. The letter is dated August 17th, 1694.

When at Scalan the Bishop had the honour of a visit from His Grace the Duke of Gordon and Mr. Menzies of Pitfodels. On the following day Bishop Chisholm arrived from the Highlands, and was introduced to the potentate of the North. From Scalan the two Bishops proceeded to Gibston, where they held the annual meeting. The greatest harmony prevailed. Bishop Hay left the choice of a new Procurator entirely to the administrators of the mission funds, having first laid before them the circumstances which, he thought, ought to determine them. He then withdrew, lest his presence should be a restraint on their deliberations, and left them to proceed with their election. They agreed unanimously to ask him to retain the office for three years longer. He had already declared, both publicly and privately, that he would perform no more the trying duties of the procuratorship. This resolution, however, was changed by the unanimous request of the administrators that he would accept the charge for another period on certain conditions.

Some time was now devoted to the preparation of the usual letters to Rome, to Propaganda, the Cardinals Albani, Carrafazajetto and Zalaga, the Secretary of State. In all these letters there was an account of the affairs of the Scotch mission. The letter to Propaganda consisted of a general statement, describing the journeys, receptions and health of each of the Bishops during the past year; and not omitting the losses sustained by the mission in France and elsewhere. The letter to Cardinal Zalada gave the most details, as he was more a stranger to the mission affairs, and estimated the number of Catholics in Scotland at 45,000.

After the meeting, Bishops Hay and Chisholm repaired by way of the Enzie to Aberdeen, where the letters to Rome were signed by all the three Bishops. Bishop Hay was very desirous, on the occasion, to see his invalid coadjutor, as appearances indicated but too plainly that it might be the last time. Bishop Chisholm was much affected. "It was a moving sight," he said, "to see the helpless invalid in the condition to which he was reduced. But his mind was as vigourous as ever."

Yielding so far to the representations of the Bishops, through the wise management of the agent, an American priest of high character was appointed confessor to the students and director of their studies. This was done notwithstanding the opposition of the Rector and his Prefect. Propaganda, at the same time, assigned two places in their College to Scotch students, and undertook to pay the travelling expenses of young priests ordained for Scotland when their relations were too poor to pay for them. More than this was desirable; but the Scotch Bishops were satisfied, in the meantime, by having obtained so much.

The Glasgow mission, as yet in its commencement, was in danger of losing ground by the appointment of Mr. McDonell, to the chaplaincy of the Glengarry regiment. His new office, however, was of such importance that the Bishop could not refuse to let him accept it. Mr. Farquarson was taken from his superintendence of the students at Aberdeen and appointed to the vacant charge.

At last there was a reconciliation of the two families of Guelph and Stewart. Prince Augustus, of the former line, was spending the summer at Grotta Ferrata, and often had occasion to meet Cardinal York. He never met him but he caused his phaeton to stop and stood with his hat in his hand till the Cardinal was passed. This repeated attention produced the effect which the Prince desired. Latterly, the Cardinal ordered his carriage to stop too, and kindly enquired after the Prince's health, expressing at the same time, his affection towards him and his friends, and how much he wished to be on the most intimate terms with *His Royal Highness*, his dear cousin. He hoped also that political disputes between their families would not now, any longer, give umbrage. The Prince was so much struck with this very friendly and unexpected show of kindness on the part of the Cardinal that he could not find words to express his feeling; but only repeated three times, *I thank your Royal Highness*. On the following day he made amends for this, and walked with the Cardinal for more than two hours. He afterwards dined with him and sought his conversation every evening. The Cardinal was delighted with the amiable qualifications of the Prince.

Bishop Geddes was still capable of extraordinary literary activity. Besides collecting what he could relating to the history of religion in Scotland, and in addition to his "Life of St. Margaret," which his nephew, Mr. Gordon, had printed at his own risk, he had lately composed a pastoral letter in Latin, addressed to the Scotch missionaries. A hundred copies of this letter were printed. He flattered himself that his contributions to the Encyclopedia might do good to religion, inasmuch as they afforded an opportunity of representing the true state of things. It had a circulation of 6000 copies, which found their way to all parts of the world. He had also finished the lives of Boscovich and Stay, together with a new life of the admirable Creighton. All of these were soon to appear in the supplement to the Encyclopedia. After mentioning these contributions, in a letter to him, Dr. Gleig said: "I read with much pleasure the account you gave me of your head and heart. Long may they continue sound; and that you may have as little pain as possible, in this world, and, when the Father of mercies shall be pleased to remove you to a better, that your departure may be easy and happy, is the sincere prayer of, Right Reverend and dear sir, your most respectful, humble servant.

GEORGE GLEIG."

It was an additional consolation to the invalid to receive a most kind letter from George Chalmers, giving him an account of many literary undertakings and projects in connection with the antiquities of Scotland and his share in them, expressing, at the same time, his warm interest in the restoration of the invalid Bishop's health.

Pecuniary embarrassment added, in no slight degree, to the patient's sufferings. The arrears due him in Spain were only in part recovered, and his debt amounted to £900. This was an evil, however, that could be removed; and Bishop Hay promptly adopted measures for its removal. He took all the debt upon himself, together with the management of whatever income the invalid possessed; and after making a reasonable allowance for maintenance, devoted the remainder to the payment of debt. Mr. McPherson, also lent his aid, and succeeded in obtaining an addition to the Bishop's income of seventy-two crowns yearly. Sir Thomas Durham had left to Propaganda, about the middle of the seventeenth century, 2,000 crowns for the support of Protestant clergymen who might become Catholics. As there were but few such conversions, the fund had been applied latterly to more general purposes. A person having died who enjoyed a pension accruing from this fund, the ever mindful agent, chiefly through the influence of Cardinal Albani, secured it for Bishop Geddes; and, after his debts were paid to the Seminaries in Scotland. Bishop Geddes was very grateful to all concerned in this business, not forgetting Cardinal Albani, whom he specially thanked.

Among the many literary occupations which engaged the attention of Bishop Geddes, his tract on duelling was not forgotten. A copy of it together with the life of St. Margaret was sent to the office of the Encyclopedia, addressed to Dr. Gleig. Bishop Hay was much impressed on reading the biography of Boscovich. "Poor man!" he said, "how I was affected with the account of his latter days. Mr. George Maxwell was no less so." Bishop Geddes' friends at Edinburgh never ceased to enquire for him. Among these were the Lord Advocate and Lord Monboddo. Mrs. Maxwell, of Kirkconnell, showed her interest by sending a bottle of the tincture of lavender, which was said to be good for paralytic affections. Needless to say it had no more effect than the kind enquiries of many friends.

The loss of the foreign Colleges rendered it necessary that the Bishops should direct their attention towards enlarging the Seminaries at home. It happened at the time that a very eligible property in the Enzie, near Gordon Castle, was for sale. The purchase had many advocates, especially Bishop Geddes. Bishop Hay dreaded the expense which it would entail. Finally, after a great deal of serious discussion, the idea of purchasing was abandoned. It would, no doubt, have been highly advantageous to have a College in such a choice locality. The vicinity of the ducal palace would have been a tower of strength, for the Dukes of Gordon, although now Protestant, inherited the ancestral will to befriend the Catholics. Duke Alexander, at that time head of the ancient House, showed his mind on the subject in a very decided and public manner. One day, at a county meeting, there arose a discussion as to the loyal dispositions of various denominations, when His Grace of Gordon, confidently said that, after a thorough examination of matters, *he would take it on himself to answer for the Roman Catholics to a man.* It was also a great recommendation of the property proposed that the majority of the surrounding population was Catholic. There was only one objection to so eligible a site for a Catholic college, the pecuniary difficulty which it would occasion.

At the commencement of 1795 there was some discussion on the subject of public prayers for the King and Royal Family. Mr. Menzies, of Pitfodels, had the introduction of such prayers much at heart; and, at his earnest request, Bishop Geddes proposed the practice to Bishop Hay. The latter was opposed to making it obligatory on the clergy; but would willingly suggest it, and leave it to them to adopt it if they chose. In Galloway the practice had become general. At Edinburgh, also, it had been begun. If Aberdeen followed these examples, the custom would, no doubt, spread in the North. As an encouragement the Bishop suggested a form of prayer which might be adopted. After mentioning the Church, her pastors and the welfare of religion, he proposed that the following words should be used: "Let us also recommend to the mercy of Almighty God, our Sovereign, King George, Charlotte, our Queen, and all the Royal Family, with all our civil magistrates and rulers under whom we live; that our good Lord may direct them in all their ways, to what is most for His glory, the good of their own souls and the establishment of His holy religion amongst us."

CAP. LIII.

BISHOP GEDDES CONTINUES HIS LITERARY LABOURS—MR. HIPPISLEY AND NATIONAL SUPERIORS—BISHOP GEDDES A PEACE MAKER—ARRIVALS FROM SPAIN—ORDINATIONS—BISHOP HAY INJURED BY A HORSE—MR. ALEXANDER INNES IMPRISONED—HOSTILE PREJUDICE DIMINISHING AT GLASGOW—BISHOP GEDDES TENDERLY CARED FOR—PECUNIARY DIFFICULTY AT GLASGOW—BISHOP HAY ABUSED—BISHOP GEDDES MAKES PEACE—HIGH OPINION OF MISSION AT ROME—PURPOSE TO HAVE A LARGER SEMINARY AT HOME—A COADJUTOR DESIRED—ALEXANDER CAMERON DIGNISSIMUS—THE SAME CHOSEN—THE ARMY LIBERAL—LIFE OF ST. MARGARET TO THE SOCIETY OF ANTIQUARIES—CLAIM OF THE BISHOPS FOR THE COLLEGE PROPERTIES IN FRANCE—THEY SEEK ADDITIONAL REPEAL OF THE PENAL LAWS—REPRINT OF THE NEW TESTAMENT—LIBERALITY OF SIR JOHN LAWSON, "THE FLOWER OF THE ENGLISH CATHOLIC GENTRY."

Bishop Geddes was still able to continue his literary labours, and with his wonted activity. Dr. Gleig alone kept him busy, and at work of the most agreeable kind. This indefatigable writer had just prepared an article on Purgatory, founding on "The Papist Misrepresented and Represented." In this essay the learned doctor showed that the doctrine was perfectly harmless and not peculiar to the Church of Rome. There appeared in a former edition of the Encyclopedia an account of Purgatory which he considered very absurd. But the doctrine he thought, when fairly stated, was exceedingly reasonable. He requested that the Bishop would write for him a short paper on canonization under the word saint, or to refer him to a good and fair account of it, such as he remembered having seen in Bishop Hay's *Scripture Doctrine of Miracles*. Dr. Gleig, moreover, consulted the Bishop in regard to the Roman Catholic view of the Real Presence in the Eucharist, which he proposed inserting under the word, transubstantiation, or the Lord's Supper. It must be owned that the non-juror's edition of the Encyclopedia Britannica freely opened its pages, with most exemplary impartiality, to a fair statement on both sides of every vexed question.

We now find diplomacy at work. Mr. Hippisley, as powerful at Rome as ever, applied with his wonted energy, to the apparently hopeless task of obtaining national superiors for the British Colleges. Mr. McPherson, as representing the Scotch Bishops, cordially seconded his endeavours. What may be called an accident, held out for some time a prospect of success. Serious disturbance occurred in the Irish College, consequent upon the misrule of its Italian masters. The students appealed to Mr. Hippisley. The diplomatist promptly took up their cause, and addressed Cardinal Livizani, the protector of the Irish. The Cardinal replied in polite terms, but not to the satisfaction of Mr. Hippisley, who, in turn, expressed his regret that his arguments had not weighed with his Eminence, adding, moreover, that "he trusted to the wisdom and justice of the venerable Sovereign whose moderation, sweetness and goodness have gained for him so much glory, and won all hearts." The British envoy lost no time in carrying the case to the Pope, pleading earnestly for Irish superiors to the College, and for justice to the students. He also addressed to Cardinal Albani, Dean of the College of Cardinals, a letter in which much kindness of heart was mingled with the politician's instinctive love of negociation and diplomacy. The vigorous appeals of Mr. Hippisley, meanwhile, backed by his threats of asking his own Government to interfere, gave, at last, a fair prospect of success to the cause for which the Bishop had been so long contending. The death of Campanelli, the English protector, destroyed this prospect. Albani and others concerned in the matter condemned the proposal to make any change. The support of Cardinal Antonelli at Propaganda was lost to the advocates of national superiors by his resignation, at the time, in consequence of his increasing infirmities. His successor, Cardinal Gerdil, although good and able, was too aged and too little acquainted with Scotch affairs efficiently to replace him. The English College, notwithstanding, obtained a sort of promise that a national superior would be appointed at the next vacancy.

Some difference having arisen between the two priests at Aberdeen and Bishop Hay, the mistrust entertained by the latter was done away with by the peace-loving Bishop Geddes, who assured the senior Bishop that there were no two clergymen in the country who had his welfare more at heart. It was a source of consolation to Bishop Geddes to contribute towards peace and unanimity.

This year (1795) Mr. Rattray and Mr. John Sharp, so favourably known afterwards in the missions, were expected from Spain; and the same year Mr. Andrew Carruthers and Mr. Andrew Scott, both, at a later date, Bishops, the former at Edinburgh and the latter at Glasgow, were ordained priests by Bishop Hay at Aberdeen. Mr. Charles Gordon, destined to be for many years the popular priest of Aberdeen, and who at the time wanted two or three months of the age required for priests' orders, was on the same occasion promoted to the rank of deacon. The day after the ordination the Bishop conducted Mr. Scott to the mission of Deeside, for which he was destined, and introduced him to the congregation. The Bishop on returning happened to pass a man who was leading a young horse, and at the moment the Bishop was passing the animal turned suddenly round and kicked him on the shin. The blow was at first very painful; but he thought nothing of it till he reached Aberdeen, when it was found to be so bad as to oblige him to keep his room for several weeks. He was thus prevented from giving any assistance with the duties of Easter-tide.

During the reign of terror in France, considerable anxiety was caused to the Bishops by the imprisonment of Mr. Alexander Innes, who had been temporarily appointed Principal of the Scotch College at Paris. When some kind of order was restored, however, he was set at liberty.

Mr. Farquarson, lately appointed to Glasgow, as successor to Mr. Alexander McDonell, gave at this time a very favourable account of the mission there. In a letter to his friend, Mr. McPherson, he stated that he had been ten days on duty in the western city. There was no lack of work; everything was quiet and prejudice was wearing off. Andrew Carruthers, recently ordained, was to be his neighbour in the mission of Drummond. There was an emigrant French priest at Glasgow, one at Dundee, one at St. Andrews, and two at Edinburgh, besides several in Galloway. They all hoped soon, on the conclusion of peace, to return to their own country. Bishop Hay, Mr. Farquarson adds, was about to repair to the North and spend the summer there. He was heartily tired of managing the pecuniary business of the mission, there being a deficit which he knew not how to make up in consequence of some losses, the late increase of missionaries and bank stock calls. He intended in three or four years to retire from office giving up all concern with the mission's money concerns. But, who would condescend, after him, to undertake the charge? In the same letter Mr. Farquarson says that Bishop Geddes could not be better cared for. His nephews are all attention to him, especially the younger of them, Mr. Chas. Gordon. One of them is constantly, day and night, beside him. Bishop Hay forwards or orders for him whatever is thought beneficial. He is greatly and almost constantly pained all over his joints, legs, thighs and arms. In a short time he will not be able to get the spoon to his mouth. His head and trunk of body are still sound. His intellectual faculties are better than ever. His appetite is rather too keen ; and he is becoming bulky and astonishingly weighty. He dictates commonly, an hour, every day, either for the Encyclopedia or the history of our missions. He is always in good humour and deems himself, in all respects, extremely happy, yet longs for death. His wishes, I assure him, being contrary to those of all others, will not be heard for some years.

The ardour of Mr. Farquarson's predecessor had carried him a little too far when at Glasgow. There were embarrassing pecuniary difficulties ; and the congregation were in danger of losing their church for arrears of rent. It was finally agreed that the rent should be reduced to £30 instead of £40. It was also decided to ask the congregation to pay this lesser sum and the rent of the priest's house, but nothing else.

It cannot but be recorded with deep regret that some of the clergy should have thought proper to speak harshly and even abusively of the venerable Bishop. That so eccentric an individual as Mr. Charles Maxwell should have done so is little to be wondered at. He appears to have been connected with a little club of censors and signed himself K. G. K. (Knight of the Gordian Knot.) He was known among his more intimate associates as "*Sir Ned.*" He wrote letters to Mr. MacPherson filled with bitter reproaches against Bishop Hay, his arbitrary measures and his overbearing temper. This Maxwell, Mr. MacPherson and Mr. Farquarson joined with a few others in censuring, and not unfrequently maligning among themselves everything that Bishop Hay undertook, all of them, however, acknowledging that his intentions were good and honest. Bishop Geddes listened to their complaints; and sometimes communicated them to the senior Bishop. But on all such occasions he strenuously laboured to maintain peace, or, at least, outward harmony. In this he was admirably successful, insomuch that the absence of public disputes among the Scotch clergy was mentioned as one of the reasons why their little church stood so high in public opinion at Rome, and so favourably contrasted with the noisy disputes which from time to time distracted the English clerical body.

The annual letter to Rome this year (1795) was dated from Aberdeen. In a letter to the Holy Father, the Bishops informed him of their purpose to establish a larger seminary at home, in order to supply for their losses in France.

In October, Bishop Hay consulted the agent at Rome, Mr. McPherson, on the subject of a coadjutor. In his reply, the agent recommended Mr. Farquarson, an ex-administrator, as a man, he humbly thought, in whom nothing was wanting to fit him for so important an office. It might be, he added, that his judgment was somewhat influenced by the sincere friendship and affection he had always entertained for the late rector of Douai College; but, he must candidly own, at the same time, that, if he were called upon to name another for the position, he should be quite at a loss. Meanwhile, the increasing illness of Bishop Geddes was rendering the question of the coadjutorship every day more pressing. In July, 1797, Bishop Hay was with his coadjutor at Aberdeen, and thence despatched letters to Propaganda on the necessity of appointing a coadjutor. He wrote, at length of the state of incapacity to which long illness had reduced Bishop Geddes, and the infirmities which age, hard and incessant labour, together with constitutional head-aches, had brought upon himself. His memory in particular, he said, was much decayed, as he found to his inconvenience when anything occurred requiring fixed attention and recollection of the past. He, in consequence, entreated the congregation of Propaganda to grant him another coadjutor, and proposed, as was the custom, three persons, as fit for the office. First was named, *dignissimus*, Alexander Cameron, rector of the Scotch College of Valladolid, whose abilities and character stood very high in the estimation of all who knew him. The second, *dignior*, was Mr. John Gordon, vice-rector of the same College, and a man of exemplary piety and of such reputation for learning as to be commonly known at Valladolid as an oracle of theological science. The third, *dignus* was Mr. Donald Stewart, an excellent and meritorious missionary priest. The persons named had been all educated at Rome ; and this, as Bishop Hay well judged, was no slight recommendation. The application was received at Rome at a time that was very unfavourable to the rapid despatch which Bishop Hay so much desired. The months of September and October were then, and are still, considered by the Romans as vacation time, on which no kind of business should intrude. All who had the means, retired to the country. The Scotch agent, notwithstanding, was so much in favour with the authorities at Propaganda, that they consented to have the matter promptly despatched, without waiting for a meeting of the congregation, *or audientia S. S. mi.* There was a marked inclination to name Mr. John Gordon, so much· were the Cardinals moved by the splendid character given to him by the Bishops. The agent, however, holding out for the selection made by the Bishops, the choice fell on Mr. Alexander Cameron, who then became Vicar-Apostolic of the

Lowland district of Scotland, with the title of Bishop of Maximianopolis, I. P. I.

It may now be placed on record, as showing the greater liberality with which our soldiers were treated, that the commandant of a fencible regiment gave orders that the men should attend the churches of their respective denominations. The Saturday after their arrival at Dundee he addressed them in the following terms: "You that are Roman Catholics divide, and stand at my right; you of the Church of England on my left; and let the Presbyterians remain where they are. You Roman Catholics will go to-morrow to the Seagate where the Roman Catholic priest, Mr. Pepper, lives; you of the Church of England to the English chapel; you of the Church of Scotland, to the Kirk. But see you go, all of you. from the parade ground, in rank and file, with a drummer and fifer at the head of each division." The name of the officer who thus acted was Colonel Baillie. Bishop Geddes, at this time, December 1795, wrote at some length to Bishop Hay notwithstanding the increased severity of his ailment. Among other things, he requested that the Bishop would send his "Life of St. Margaret" to the Society of Antiquaries. The signature, the only part of the letter in his own hand writing, is weak and unsteady, still, however, retaining much of the character of his old style.

As the English Bishops had applied for restitution through the British Government of their properties at Paris and Douai, with the best hopes of success in the event of peace being concluded between the two countries, there was no reason why the Bishops in Scotland should not make a similar application. The Lord Advocate and Mr. Henry Dundas, whom they first addressed on the subject, returned a very favourable answer and promised to keep their application in mind when the proper time came. They also memorialized Mr. Brodie, M. P., on the subject of their losses which they estimated at 30,000 livres of annual income. They, at the same time, directed the attention of this gentleman to another grievance for which they sought redress. Their fellow-Catholics in England, according to the recent Act, repealing so far the penal laws, were now free to erect seminaries at home for the education of youth. By some oversight, however, in the Scotch Act, the clause which was intended to prohibit them from educating the children of Protestaut parents, was so worded as to amount to a prohibition against their educating their own children.

For some years there had been a great demand among the Catholics of Scotland for copies of the Scriptures, particularly the New Testament, in English. So far back as 1790 Bishop Geddes spoke of this matter to Bishop Hay on which occasion the Bishop suggested that Dr. Challoner's New Testament, at least, should be reprinted. To meet the expenses of such a reprint, Sir John Lawson, of Brough, whom Bishop Geddes described as *the flower of the English Catholic gentry*, offered to subscribe £50 on condition of Bishop Geddes superintending it. Mr. Robertson, a Benedictine priest of Ratisbon, would willingly undertake the editorial drudgery. Bishop Hay was satisfied that a great demand for the English Scriptures had existed for eight or ten years previously. In 1782 he had consulted Chalmers, the Aberdeen printer, about a reprint. Chalmers, after a few days' consideration, offered to reprint for £250 an edition of the whole Bible in every respect similar to the London edition, so that the four volumes of the Old Testament might be sold at 5s. bound. The Bishop was well pleased with the coadjutor's proposal to have a reprint, but his financial condition would not allow him to advance any money. With the aid of Sir John Lawson's subscription, however, Bishop Geddes was enabled to commence the work of reprinting the New Testament. He was resolved that the type, paper and binding, should be good, as everything connected with religion ought to be; and he hoped to see it sold at 2s. It was his intention to follow Bishop

Challoner's edition with as few alterations as possible. Bishop Hay was particularly averse to changes, whether in the text or in the notes. People had been long accustomed, he said, to Bishop Challoner's edition, and they might be startled at finding alterations. More than this, Benedict XIV., in his preface to the *Index Expurgatorius*, made honourable mention of the translation. This was some sanction, surely, the Bishop thought, although not a formal document.

www.ingramcontent.com/pod-product-compliance
Lightning Source LLC
Chambersburg PA
CBHW020810230426
43666CB00007B/945